HEROES, HAIRBANDS AND HISSY FITS

Chappers' Modern History of Football

HEROES, HAIRBANDS AND HISSY FITS

Chappers' Modern History of Football

Mark Chapman

BANTAM PRESS

LONDON · TORONTO · SYDNEY · AUCKLAND · JOHANNESBURG

TRANSWORLD PUBLISHERS
61–63 Uxbridge Road, London W5 5SA
A Random House Group Company
www.rbooks.co.uk

First published in Great Britain
in 2010 by Bantam Press
an imprint of Transworld Publishers

Images courtesy of Alamy, p73; Getty Images, p9; Press Association
Images p99, 141, 173, 205, 247; Splash News p45

A CIP catalogue record for this book
is available from the British Library.

ISBN 9780593064269

Addresses for Random House Group Ltd companies outside the UK
can be found at: www.randomhouse.co.uk
The Random House Group Ltd Reg. No. 954009

The Random House Group Limited supports the Forest Stewardship Council
(FSC), the leading international forest-certification organization. All our titles that
are printed on Greenpeace-approved FSC-certified paper carry the FSC logo. Our
paper procurement policy can be found at www.rbooks.co.uk/environment

Typeset in 11.5/16pt Minion by
Falcon Oast Graphic Art Ltd.
Printed and bound in Great Britain by
CPI Mackays, Chatham, ME5 8TD

2 4 6 8 10 9 7 5 3 1

Mixed Sources
Product group from well-managed
forests and other controlled sources
www.fsc.org Cert no. TT-COC-2139
© 1996 Forest Stewardship Council
FSC

For Ben and Jessie
(or Eric and Ole Gunnar
as they should have been called)

Contents

Introduction   1

The Kit
Shirts and Shorts   11
Skins   17
The Ball   22
Socks   29
Hairbands   35
Boots   40

The Player
Footballers   47
The House   51
WAGs   58
Autobiographies   61
Squad Numbers   65

The Grounds
Identikit Stadia   75
Away Fans   82
Products on Sale   89
Moving Advertising Boards   93

The Game
Tackling 101
Diving 108
Injuries 115
Goal Celebrations 124
Trophy Presentations 134

The Fans
Quiet Fans 143
Chants 149
Tourist Fans 156
Newcastle Fans 162
The England Band 168

The Manager
Owners and Directors 175
Press Conferences 179
Pre- and Post-Match Interviews 185
Media Bans 189
Dress Sense 194
Headsets 199

The Authorities
The Referee 207
The 4th Official 216
Sepp Blatter 223
The Premier League 231
Tournament Draws 238

The Media
The Phone-In 249
Journalists' Exclusives! 258
Club Media 262

Press Officers   267
Sky Sports News   269
Pundits   276
Fantasy Football   280
DVDs   284
Books   287

Epilogue   290
Index   299

Introduction

When I raise my eyes from the computer screen in front of me and look at the wall directly behind, I see a picture frame. It is the size of an A4 piece of paper, and it contains two objects that are incredibly precious to me. These objects have shaped the past twenty-eight years of my life, and they only cost £1.40 each.

If I leave my desk and head upstairs, I'll probably trip over two pairs of football boots. One is adult's, size 10. They are classic black and look like they are made of leather. They have proper circular screw-in studs on their soles. Next to them is a pair of children's size 1 boots. They are a garish orange, look like they are made of plastic, and instead of screw-in studs they have 'blades'.

At the top of the stairs, I can turn into my seven-year-old boy's bedroom. On the wall, by the light switch, is a picture frame. It is the size of an A4 piece of paper, and it contains two objects that in years to come might become incredibly precious to him. They could even shape the rest of his life. They cost £55 each.

My two tickets are mounted on red cardboard, and printed underneath them in bold black type is 'the first time . . . october 1981'. (It is only now, when a red line appears under October on my screen, that I realize my dad made an error and should have put a capital letter at the beginning of the month.)

You never ever forget your first time though, do you?

Mine was three days before my eighth birthday. I had started to follow Manchester United the year before. My first footballing memory was watching them lose to Ipswich on *Match of the Day*. If you are under eighteen and reading this, I should tell you that both Manchester United and *Match of the Day* were very different back then. United weren't much good and *Match of the Day* was never abbreviated to *MOTD*. The programme didn't show all the day's goals, and normally only featured two or three matches, so it was a real treat when your club was on. It also had television's biggest graphics. None of these little bars in the top left-hand corner with the teams abbreviated and the letters in the colours of the kit. Oh no. When the score was put on the screen in 1980 you could no longer see the actual game.

United lost to Ipswich in that game on *MOTD* – sorry, *Match of the Day*, but the United goalkeeper had saved a penalty, and so it was that on 8 October 1981 I walked up to Old Trafford in a generic green goalkeeping top, with pimpled goalkeeping gloves on my hands, wanting to be Gary Bailey. My dad was with me, as were three of my mates, one of whom had the biggest red, white and black scarf I'd ever seen. When we all sat down on our wooden seats the scarf stretched across the five us. Now this could be because it was a genuinely long scarf, or it could be because the seats were packed a lot closer together in 1981.

As I left Old Trafford after the game that evening, I didn't want to be Gary Bailey any more. Nor did I want to be Sammy McIlroy, who had hit a hat-trick in the 5–0 thrashing of Wolves. I didn't even want to be George Berry, the visitor's big centre-half who had the best haircut I had ever seen in my life. If he had been bald he would have been 6'2"; thanks to his afro he was at least 7'1". No, I wanted to be the young man with the curly perm who signed for my club just before kick-off.

This wasn't a signing that took place in the bowels of the stadium before the world's media, with the player, the manager and the director of football sat in front of two huge boards plastered with the club's sponsors or 'global partners'. This signing took place on an uncovered trestle table placed on the pitch. It wasn't in the centre circle where everybody could see, but beside one touchline, so that three-quarters of the fans had to crane their necks to make anything out, and even then they would have only seen the top of a perm. There were a few photographers, but certainly not hordes of camera crews from international sports broadcasters and twenty-four-hour news channels. As Bryan Robson put pen to paper to break the British transfer record, I had found my boyhood hero. Remi Moses also signed for the club at the same time, but he never had quite the same effect on me.

Over the next twelve and a half years, Robbo captained United, dislocated his shoulder, scored the fastest ever

England goal at a World Cup, dislocated his shoulder, was carried off the pitch by jubilant fans after an amazing United comeback against Barcelona, dislocated his shoulder, won the FA Cup, sank a few pints, dislocated his shoulder, won another FA Cup, then dislocated his shoulder. Bryan Robson could do no wrong for me. I lived and breathed United, and I wanted to be Captain Marvel.

I still wish I was Bryan Robson, which is hard to admit when you're a thirty-something man. I actually got to meet him a few years ago, although not by using my contacts as a sports presenter and journalist. I met him through desperately needing a piss at a charity dinner.

As I unzipped and popped the little fella out, I looked to my left. There, standing next to me, was Bryan Robson. I immediately turned away and followed the strict urinal rules of staring straight ahead and making no eye contact, but my mind was in turmoil. Should I strike up a conversation? What could I say to him? 'Hi Bryan, I know you are having a piss at the moment, but your goal in the FA Cup replay against Liverpool at Maine Road was one of the best moments of my life.' Should I try and shake his hand? 'Listen, Bryan, I just have to shake your hand, so could you pop your todger in your other one for just a second?' Should I ask for his autograph? If I did that though, what would he think I was asking him to sign? Should I take a sneaky peek? It was tempting, I have to admit.

The problem was that all this turmoil was causing me so much anxiety, I couldn't actually go. So while Robbo was happily gushing away next to me (I'm assuming he had a few pints to get rid of), I was just stood there, tackle out, nothing happening. He finished, washed his hands and left. My opportunity had gone.

And I didn't take a peek, before you ask.

Fast forward to April 2007, and I am again in a public convenience. (Frankly, I'm slightly concerned how many of my life reference points seem to be toilet-related.) I have taken my four-year-old son to the loos at Villa Park ten minutes before the FA Cup semi-final between Manchester United and Watford kicks off, in a vain attempt to make sure that he doesn't need to go seven minutes into the match.

Ben's speciality is to wait until something starts and then suddenly need to go to the loo. He is under the impression that I am the human equivalent of Sky Plus, and can pause any event we are at so that he can do this. Brian Conley in panto, *Shrek 3* and Girls Aloud at Wembley Arena were all ruined by him not being able to control his bladder. Well, I didn't want him to miss his first ever goal at a live game, which is why we found ourselves struggling at a urinal in the frenzied minutes leading up to kick-off. And that is one of my two memories from that afternoon.

The other is driving away from the game and having fish and chips with an ecstatic four-year-old boy. He told me how lucky we were that we supported the team that won 4–1, how much he loved Wayne Rooney and Cristiano Ronaldo, and that he didn't ever EVER want to take his United shirt off. His memories of his first football game were now lodged in his head, and, like me, I hope he never loses them.

Yet I can hardly remember anything about my son's first

game. I just had to go on to soccerbase.com to check the final score. My son is falling in love with the greatest sport on earth, just as I am starting to question it. When I was growing up I was bemused by men who fondly reminisced about a heavy ball held together by laces, and that the mark of a true winger was to make sure the ball was crossed so that the laces didn't land on the forehead of the centre-forward. I was bemused by men moaning about the ever-decreasing length of footballers' shorts and the ever-increasing length of their hair, and confused when they complained that players were getting too much money.

Have I now turned into one of those men? Should I now be wearing a cloth cap and muttering that 'it isn't as good as it were in my day', or has the game really lost its magic? Football remains the people's game. It still stirs emotions in me that nothing else can. But just why is so much of it so so so BLOODY ANNOYING?

There are some things that we have to accept about the modern game because we can't really do anything about them. Some people would describe it as progress. It would be easy to write pages and pages lamenting the effect that money has had on the game, but we can't fight that. Footballers and those involved in football have always been richer than the generation before. There were old duffers in the 1980s moaning that players earned £150,000 a year; now there are old duffers moaning that players earn £150,000 a week. When Ben reaches old duffer stage he'll probably be moaning that players earn £150,000 a day.

While the media and the journalists and the pundits write

and speak about the evils of money, the influence of foreign owners and the debts incurred by so many clubs, the fans down the pub have much more worthwhile things to discuss. What number shirt will the new signing get? Why have we signed a player who wears an alice band? Why can't the bloke in charge of the FA Cup draw read an autocue? Why do football phone-ins take so many calls from nobheads? Why do referees wear headsets? Sepp Blatter – why? Why does Gallas wear number 10?

Yes, we should all be grateful that we have football, and that every weekend we can watch some of the best games in the world. But this is a book about those things that irritate me in the modern game. Maybe we, the fans, can even try and change them. So vent your anger with me, moan with me, and if you think I'm just an old duffer who should be wearing a cloth cap, you can shout at me too.

THE
KIT

....

Shirts and Shorts

'Only the crumbliest, flakiest Chapman' was a chant that was regularly heard on my school playground in South Manchester during the 1980s. Sung to the tune of the Cadbury's Flake television advert, it was aimed in my direction virtually every playtime. I had to endure the wit of my fellow pupils because I suffered from very dry skin. This was partly down to my eczema as a baby, and partly to the Admiral England home kit that was worn in the 1982 World Cup.

As a design, I absolutely loved that kit. It was white, with red and blue stripes running across both shoulders. It looked fantastic. Unfortunately, it might as well have been made out of barbed wire for all the comfort it gave me. It irritated, it itched, and it made me scratch and scratch and scratch. And the more I scratched, the more my skin fell off, and the more the other kids compared me to a crumbly chocolate bar.

To my knowledge, Admiral never advertised the '82 kit with the slogan 'Makes you look great but feel shit', but nowadays every single kit has to be marketed and launched.

It is not enough for sportswear manufacturers to just let the fans buy the latest strip. They are under the impression that now supporters will only put their hands in their pockets if they detail how the kit has been made. And by that I don't mean tell them it was made in a Chinese sweatshop for the price of a packet of crisps. Oh no. They try and blind us with science.

Every kit now has the 'latest technology', 'tested by astronauts on their last moonwalk', and will probably have 'interwoven stitching' in its 'clima-cool fabric'. The upshot of all this is that with every new kit, you'll sweat less. You could be clinically obese and wearing it on the beach in Torremolinos in 100-degree heat, yet thanks to the latest technology there won't be one drop of perspiration.

Science has become the holy grail of kit manufacturers. Yet, despite all their claims, most footballers still leave the pitch dripping with sweat – with the exception of Dimitar Berbatov, and I'm fairly sure that's because he doesn't run.

Sweat has become the kit fad of our time. In the early 1990s the trend was to see who could have the baggiest shorts. This was welcome, especially to those of us who had been virtually castrated by the shorts of the 1980s. It was so easy for Vinnie Jones to find Paul Gascoigne's testicles in that famous photograph because the Newcastle shorts of the time presented them on a plate. It's a wonder that those of us in our thirties have managed to produce children.

The next trend was for shirts to have tassels. Aston Villa and Manchester United were just two of the clubs to have lace-up shirts, as kits were taken back to the start of the twentieth century. I thought they looked great, until I tried to play in one of them. After one particularly explosive run, the little plastic thing on the end of the piece of string smacked me in the mouth and nearly took out my front teeth. I continued to wear the shirt, but never ran quite so explosively again.

Once we entered the twenty-first century, manufacturers began turning to science. And it is here that I have to single out two companies in particular: Kappa and Nike.

Kappa were responsible for the worst kit invention of all time, the skin-tight shirt. They made it for Spurs, Wales and Italy. In their design meeting it probably seemed like a good idea. 'It would mean an end to shirt pulling because there would be nothing to get hold of, and at the same time the number of women watching the game will increase because they would be watching toned athletes in figure-hugging shirts.' Or at least that's how I imagine one bloke in a suit sold it to the rest of the room while standing next to an overhead projector. What somebody else in that room should then have piped up with is 'But what about John Hartson?' And then somebody else should have interjected with 'And what about the fans?' The skin-tight design was a disaster for anyone without a six-pack. It somehow managed to make Hartson look even bigger than he was, and fans who thought they could get away with wearing the replica shirts quickly realized they couldn't. Skin-tight tops and beer bellies are not an attractive combination.

While Kappa were going with the skin-tight look, Nike opted for an inner shirt inside the actual top. Why? Because they believed this would help the player sweat less, with the inner layer taking most of the perspiration and leaving the shirt itself apparently sweat-free. The actual result of this design was to make Diego Forlan look like a nob. His Manchester United goals were few and far between, so when he got one he wanted to celebrate. When the Uruguayan got the winner in a Premier League game against Southampton he, to use a technical term, 'went off on one'. He sprinted towards one of the corners at the Stretford End, taking his shirt off and twirling it around his head in the process, as if he was going to lasso one of the supporters. Having displayed his tanned, toned and disturbingly smooth torso to the whole of Old Trafford, Forlan proceeded to do an impression of a two-year-old who is learning how to dress himself. The game kicked off with him still unable to get his shirt back over his head. Rather than stand there and work out the complexities of the two-layered kit, Forlan kept the shirt in his hand and played topless for the next minute or so, even managing to tackle a bewildered James Beattie in the process.

When people come up with these pointless innovations, they just can't keep quiet about them. Oh no. They want to shout about them from the rooftops, or rather shout about them from the plush surroundings of a hotel meeting room. So every new kit is now accompanied by the excruciatingly God-awful experience that is the kit launch.

I once had the honour of hosting one of these kit launches, and it was no minor kit either: it was an England kit launch, in a hotel meeting room in Manchester. In my naivety I assumed I would turn up in my ill-fitting suit, stand in front of a lectern and introduce a few uncomfortable-looking footballers wearing the new kit. Instead, what I had to do was turn up in my ill-fitting suit, stand in front of a lectern and deliver a speech worthy of Stephen Hawking. I had given up physics when my skin was still crumbling, yet here I was with a script that had several words beginning with 'poly', even more words ending in 'ethane', and more references to climate control than an Al Gore film. All I really wanted to tell the room of assembled journalists and competition winners was that the kit looked nice, and all they really cared about was whether it had a gold star on it above the badge, to show that we really had once won the World Cup.

After stumbling through my ten-minute address, I then had to introduce the few uncomfortable-looking footballers. Unfortunately, by then you couldn't actually see the kit, because the organizers had pumped so much bloody dry ice on to the stage you couldn't see more than six inches in front of you. I was meant to interview David Beckham, but I had to wait for at least five minutes until he had stopped coughing and the dry ice had left the back of his throat. The interview wasn't a success either because rather than ask him about football, I had to ask him about the technology of the new strip. It was like Dumb and Dumber presents *Tomorrow's World*.

Of course not every kit is launched in a whirl of dry ice and crap presentations. A lot of kits are now unveiled at the end of a season. I'm not too keen on this either. When I watch the matches on the final day of the season I spend more time trying to work out whether a side is wearing their new strip than watching the match itself. This is particularly true when watching Everton, who seem to think a new kit design just involves adding a bit more blue or an extra dash of white.

I absolutely adore football kits, and there isn't a fan I know who doesn't share my enthusiasm. I don't care how often they are changed, how many kits each side has or how garish the designs are. They can be simple or complicated, they can make us long for a bygone age or remember a golden period in our club's history. There are strips that we thought were amazing at the time that now just look horrendous, and strips that looked horrendous at the time but are now viewed as retro and cool. They are looked down upon by fashionistas, but give me a good football strip over a Giorgio Armani jacket any day.

They matter so much to us supporters because they give us our identity. Arsenal fans were quite rightly angry with their home strip for the 2008/09 season because there was not enough white on the sleeves, and it made them look a bit like Charlton. These things matter to us. We don't want to be blinded by science or technology. We don't care if we sweat in them, or even what happens to that sweat. When we wear our club's strip we just want to look like our heroes and imagine that we are playing for our team. Beer belly or no beer belly.

Skins

Dick Crotty was a kind, genial, intelligent man. He was tall and in good shape for his age, which I would assume was late fifties or early sixties. It looked like a frisbee had been put on his head and all the hair under the frisbee had been removed, leaving tufts of wispy black hair with hints of grey at the back and above both ears. As is the case with most men of that age, the tufts of wispy black hair with hints of grey were starting to sprout out of his ears as well as above them. He probably had the greatest influence on my football 'career' and my love of the game, and to my eternal shame I have no idea whether, in 2010, he is alive or dead.

It is over twenty years since I left Brooklands Youth FC, and from the age of eight to sixteen I was coached by Mr Crotty (we never called him Dick, out of respect). He encouraged, he coached, and he once gave me the biggest bollocking I ever received when I tripped him up when he was clean through in a five-a-side game. I couldn't have been more than thirteen and I was already a dirty little git. My first touch, my ability to head a ball, my awareness, my right foot, my left foot and my ability to play the offside trap, all are down to him. Team-mates past and present are more likely to say that Mr Crotty is to blame for all of that.

He also taught me one other thing about the game, and it is something I still carry out to this day. 'Never ever wear anything under your shirt' was one of his most important rules. Our kit was a black and yellow striped shirt with black shorts and black socks. It was a kit that all mums were grateful for as they didn't need to do a Daz Doorstep Challenge on the shorts and the socks to find out how clean they had got them. The stripes on the shirt were vertical, with a black V-neck collar that delved deeply into the shirts. It meant that if you had anything on underneath your shirt, it was visible. And this was Mr Crotty's problem. A T-shirt under your strip would look messy. We also wouldn't all look the same if some of us had T-shirts on. We wouldn't look like a team. If you wanted to wear something underneath your shirt you wouldn't be in the team. It could be minus eight in January on a snow-covered pitch and you might want an extra layer underneath your cheap nylon strip to keep the chill out, but if you dared to do that you would be on the bench, getting even colder.

It was important that we didn't look like a group of individuals, but that we looked like a team. It is a theory that Arsenal employed between 2002 and 2005, although I am fairly sure they didn't get the idea from the mean streets of South Manchester and a middle-aged football coach. They used 'Captain's Call', a system where, before a game, the skipper chose whether they were to wear short sleeves or long sleeves. Whatever he decided, the whole team had to follow suit. If the captain was hard and you were a bit soft it was just tough luck that you had to wear short sleeves away to Blackburn in November in the driving rain. Mr Crotty and Arsène Wenger are obviously kindred spirits.

If Mr Crotty was in charge of Manchester United at the moment then Wayne Rooney wouldn't be getting a game, because Rooney is one of the main protagonists in a craze sweeping football. Skins.

Rooney, like many players, is a fan of wearing a tight lycra top under his shirt. At the end of the game he removes his outer layer and walks off the pitch with sweat-drenched lycra clinging to his body. Why? My first thought was that he had some unseemly blemish that he wanted to keep hidden from the world. However, having seen him jumping off yachts on holiday with Coleen he has nothing embarrassing to hide, apart from being a bit pasty, a bit hairy and not having a perfectly toned six-pack. But that doesn't stop the rest of us.

Before writing this little section, I assumed the only benefits of these kind of garments could be seen in an Eric Prydz video, so I decided I had to do some more research. No, I didn't watch 'Call on Me' non-stop for hours. That would be too tiring. Instead I went on to the Skins website to find out more.

Now, you are already aware of my distrust of science in sport and my opinion that I think most of it is just, well, commercial bollocks, and that was my position when I logged on. According to the Skins homepage, the sportswear will 'enhance your performance in training, competition and recovery', not to mention 'reduce lactic acid build-up, increase muscle oxygenation and enhance circulation'. At the same time it will 'focus muscle power' and 'prevent odour through antibacterial treatments'. And there was you thinking it was just a tight top. I am not going to doubt any of these claims, firstly because I have no scientific background or knowledge, and secondly, and more importantly, I don't want to be sued.

My research for this section actually went further than just sitting at a computer, surfing away. I decided to wear something under my own football shirt for the first time since before I was eight. My admittedly average amateur football career has taken me from Brooklands Youth FC to Hull University FC to a side called Nations on a Sunday morning. That was followed by a brief spell at Aston Boys (a very badly named side considering the entire team was over twenty-five), and finally to Ibis FC. Mr Crotty's rules have stuck with me through all those teams and my shirt has become the most important part of my kit. My only football superstition is to put my shirt on last. Indeed, when Paul Ince was in his pomp at Manchester United and I was in my pomp at Hull Uni, I copied him by not putting my shirt on until I reached the pitch. I ended that practice after an away game at Salford University in February when the changing rooms were around a mile away from the pitch. It meant that by the time I reached it I had frostbite on my nipples.

So, here I was in a changing room in West London, my white and blue Ibis shirt on the peg, about to wear something under it for the first time ever. It wasn't a Skins shirt though, it was a very tight vest that my agent had got hold of. It was a prototype and not yet on the market. She knew not to blind me with science when she gave it to me, but she did tell me that the unique selling point of the vest was that it 'would hold my belly in'. I had thought that the Ibis kit had been getting a bit smaller recently so I was happy to give this thing a go. Would it make me play like Wayne Rooney?

Would it arse. I wore the blooming thing in the warm-up and could hardly breathe. It was either very tight or my belly was very big, but I could feel my circulation start to tighten. It was off before we had even kicked off. Actually, it was off just after we had kicked off because it took a while to extricate my heaving, sweaty body from such a tight piece of clothing.

From that moment on I discovered new respect for the players who wear these things. Before my own uncomfortable experience, I used to think, 'Wazza, why are you wearing a short-sleeved shirt with a long-sleeved Skin underneath? If you're cold, why don't you just wear a long-sleeved shirt to start with?' Now I know differently. Now I know that you need a physique to carry this thing off in the first place. You actually need muscles in place for the science to work rather than just flab, and at the end of the game you come off looking sweaty but not smelling sweaty.

There are, then, obviously plenty of benefits to these things, but Mr Crotty still wouldn't approve.

The Ball

One look into my garden and there will be only one thing you will notice. It won't be the dreadfully kept lawn, which really is no longer a lawn, more a patch of mud with some tufts of grass poking through. It won't be the two bushes and some lavender that are my nod at trying to grow plants, and it won't be the decking, which I thought would bring us some alfresco living but in reality is a bugger to keep clean and probably has several rats living underneath it. The only thing you will notice is that there are balls everywhere, in particular footballs.

'How many balls does a small boy and a thirty-something man desperately trying to hang on to his youth need?' you may ask. Indeed that question is frequently asked in our house. The answer is, you can never have enough balls. (I am going to try to make sure this section has as little innuendo in it as possible, but it might be a struggle.)

In our garden at this very moment, glistening in the sunshine, I can see the OFFICIAL ball for the Champions League Final in Moscow 2008, the OFFICIAL ball for the

Premier League from a couple of seasons ago, the OFFICIAL ball used in the 2007 Champions League, the OFFICIAL ball from the 2006 World Cup in Germany, the OFFICIAL ball from the 2005 Carling Cup Final, and the OFFICIAL ball from the 2002 World Cup in Japan and South Korea. There are others but they are in neighbours' gardens after I failed to impress my son with my keepy-ups, and I use that as my argument for why we have so many footballs: my touch is dreadful, therefore we need a ready supply for when I accidentally leather one on to next-door's barbecue. In reality, though, I am weak and I allow my son to persuade me he needs the latest ball. If he is re-creating a Champions League game, he needs the OFFICIAL Champions League ball. Ditto if it is a Premier League game taking place on our twenty foot by eight foot patch of mud. I am exactly the kind of parent who is a football manufacturer's dream. They bring out a new ball for each competition and I end up buying it.

There is obviously a lot of money to be made by being a maker of footballs, and I should know because I'm doing an awful lot to help them get rich. However, they don't claim that each new ball released is a money-making scheme. Oh no. Just like the kits, each new ball is a scientific breakthrough.

When Nike launched their ball for the 2008/09 Premier League season (I can only assume that is one which has gone over the fence because I can't see it in the garden), they described it as 'the most consistent ball ever'. Does that mean all the other balls I have ever played with have been inconsistent? It would certainly explain my inability to control most of them. And the bollocks – sorry, science didn't stop there. Nike also claimed 'it had been engineered to set new standards of accuracy and visibility'. There was a '360-degree sweet spot', and the way the hexagonal and pentagonal panels fitted together created 'a nearly perfect sphere'. A *nearly* perfect sphere? You would assume that a ball that had been two years in the making and had involved computer simulations and research labs would at least be round.

Apologies if I am blinding you with science here, but there's more. This ball, or to give it its proper name the Nike Total 90 Omni Ball, had a massive red stripe across it. I assumed this was to make it look nice, but not for the first time I was wrong. 'The new red asymmetrical band encircling the ball generates a more powerful visual signal as it rotates, providing a quicker read on ball location, spin rate, speed and trajectory from any angle. It's designed to help athletes make better decisions at top-speed, when the pressure is on.' Who would have thought that a red stripe could make such a difference? Having watched Nani during the 2008/09 season, the red stripe had no effect on his awful decision-making, and the whole of the Newcastle back four seemed to struggle with ball location, red stripe or no red stripe.

Colour has suddenly become a big thing with footballs. A few years ago, a yellow ball was introduced for the winter months of the English season. The logic behind this was that it would be easier to see for players and spectators alike as the nights drew in and the rain came down. White balls, you understand, are so difficult to pick out. Yet in this bright new technicolor world of football one colour seems to have disappeared. Orange.

This may seem a strange concept if you are under twenty-five, but football used to be played in the snow. Preparing a pitch to be played in cold weather nowadays involves some quite sophisticated techniques – too sophisticated for me to understand, as my lawn will testify, although I do know it involves turning on the undersoil heating. Back in the seventies and eighties, preparing a pitch in the snow didn't rely on technical advances. It relied on a shovel. The snow would be cleared from areas of the pitch, leaving the touch-lines, penalty area and centre circle visible on a soft, clean, white blanket. Obviously I am romanticizing somewhat to make me sound more literary. It is highly unlikely that the pitch would have been soft. It was more likely rock hard and rutted and incredibly dangerous, and the snow wouldn't be clean and white, it would be slushy and a worrying brown hue. This 'picture perfect' setting would be completed by an orange ball.

Just like the Queen Mother in her later years, or a communist dictator in ill health, the orange ball was rarely seen so it always felt really special to watch a game that took place with one. It seemed more magical to my young eyes. There was more glamour for a player in smashing a brightly coloured spherical object into a net than a plain white one. Dickensian children fighting over a Christmas pudding is a traditional festive scene, but give me eighties footballers in ill-fitting shorts fighting over an orange ball as a Christmas card any day.

Unfortunately, you can't view everything in the past through rose-tinted glasses and there are some things that everybody connected to football should feel sorrow, if not shame, at, and in this case it is connected to the ball itself.

Jeff Astle was an international-class centre-forward. He scored 168 goals in 395 league games. He won five caps for England and is known by West Brom fans as 'The King'. He won the FA Cup for the club in 1968. He was a proper foot-baller, yet his daughter Dawn has said, 'At the end of the day, the game he lived for was what killed him.'

Astle died in January 2002 at the age of fifty-nine and eleven months. An inquest later revealed that he had suffered a 'brain injury consistent with repeated minor trauma'. This had been caused by Astle heading the ball during his career. The balls that Astle was connecting with were large and brown and made of leather. If it rained they would absorb water and get even heavier, reportedly 20 per cent heavier. Astle himself would describe it as heading 'a bag of bricks'. The sheer weight of the ball wasn't the end of it though. Keeping the brown leather object together were laces. If your head connected with the laces then the pain would be even worse.

Astle's mentor when he was at Notts County was Tommy Lawton. Lawton was another all-action centre-forward, and he claimed that when he played for England, the crossing of Stanley Matthews was so good and so accurate that when the ball arrived on Lawton's head Matthews would have made sure that the laces were on the opposite side, thus minimizing the pain.

After Astle stopped playing, the balls began to change. The heavy leather was replaced by lighter synthetic material, and for that professional and amateur players should all be grateful.

Each new ball launch, as I explained earlier, is now all about the science behind it. But there is another noise that accompanies the arrival of the latest ball, and that is the sound of goalkeepers complaining.

Once a ball is made for a tournament a whole batch of them are delivered to the squads taking part for them to train with. As soon as the first practice session is over you can guarantee that the goalkeepers will be moaning. Their complaint will always be the same: the new ball is 'moving too much in the air'. I am no scientist, but isn't the point of the ball to move through the air? And if it does swerve a bit then keepers do now have massive gloves on their hands that the ball should stick to. I think it is just an easy excuse to cover the fact that a lot of goalkeepers appear to have lost the art of being able to catch.

Having played with a lot of these balls, I can confirm that they do all move through the air. Usually straight into next-door's garden. I can't honestly say that one of them swerves a lot more than any of the others, and none of them moves about as much as one of the first footballs I used to have.

It cost 99p from the newsagent, came in a string basket, and was made up of black and white hexagons. They weren't referred to as panels back then. On each white hexagon was written one of the names of the twenty-two teams in the First Division. Swansea, Stoke and Brighton were alongside Ipswich, Aston Villa and Liverpool (they were the three big teams at the time), and when you kicked it you had no idea where it was going to end up. It would swerve and bounce and bobble, and if it was caught by a gust of wind it could end up five hundred yards away from you. You couldn't play a game with it, it was highly impractical, yet it was my favourite ever ball. Also, manufacturers take note, it was spherical. Completely and utterly round. Until it landed on a rose bush. Goalkeepers today should think themselves lucky they aren't facing my 99p special.

Socks

John Terry is held up as a shining example of a true England footballer. Well, on the pitch at least. OK, so after he missed the penalty that could have won Chelsea the 2008 Champions League Final against Manchester United he cried like a . . . well, he cried like I did when Matt Follas was crowned the winner of *Masterchef* in 2009 (to be fair, he had been on an incredible journey and every spoonful of every meal he created was a taste sensation). But apart from that Terry is tough and hard and passionate. In fact, missing the penalty actually added to him fitting the true England footballer stereotype.

If you Google 'John Terry' and 'brave', you get 190,000 entries. 'John Terry is a brave lion-heart of a man' according to the *Mirror*. 'Brave John Terry' is the title of an article on Soccerblog, followed by 'Our beloved John Terry scored the England winner five minutes from time'. Injuries don't affect him either. He plays through the pain. The *Guardian* once wrote, 'An ailment as trifling as a medial ligament knock would not keep England's brave John Terry on the sidelines', although being the *Guardian* it was actually written as a 'medial ligament knack'.

John Terry, or rather JT, was our England captain until the start of 2010. His blood runs blue when he plays for Chelsea and red and white when he plays for his country, and he will spill it gladly in the cause of both. Just like Stuart Pearce did when he tried to 'run off' a broken leg, JT will play through the pain barrier. He is a centre-half of the sleeves-rolled-up, fist-pumping variety. He doesn't do the fancy dan stuff. He can leather the ball the length of the pitch or clear it into the top tier of a stand. He loves a header. He's a cockney boy made good. To the Chelsea fans he is one of them. He shouts, he screams, he leads, he clatters opposition strikers, he is rough and tough and hard as nails, and yet . . . and yet he wears his socks like a girl.

Up until I was fifteen, the only thing I bothered about was football. It was the only thing that mattered morning, noon and night. And then my hormones kicked in and girls were no longer annoying and things that you could kick a football at. They were mysterious and alluring. Whereas all the fifteen-year-old boys I knew smelt of BO and were experimenting with bum fluff (facial hair would be too kind a description), the girls were smelling of perfume and conditioner and were experimenting with make-up. And on top of that, the more exotic girls on the 41 bus home from school every day would be wearing long socks that went over their knees and stopped six inches below their skirt. The winding journey through Rusholme, Fallowfield and Northenden passed quickly for hormonal boys who just stared at the hormonal girls and the tantalizing bit of leg they had on show. I didn't realize there was a curry mile in Rusholme until I left school because I had never looked out of the window.

Now, gawping at female schoolfriends' legs on the back of the number 41 bus may not equate to the moment when Elizabeth Bennet sees Mr Darcy coming out of the lake, but it was an important stage in my life and does bring back some happy memories of my sexual awakening. (I won't give any more details.) And now they have been ruined by our big lummox of an England defender. Why does he pull his socks over his knees so that they stop six inches below his shorts, thus leaving an in-no-way-tantalizing bit of flesh on show? I do not know the answer, but I do know who I blame – Thierry Henry.

In the interests of research, I have spent many hours looking at the socks – and, I suppose, legs – of football players and I can't find anybody who went for the over-the-knee look before Henry. It was something he seemed to develop during his Arsenal career. Certainly I have found no evidence of him doing it earlier in his career at either Monaco or Juventus. Maybe his first trip to Bolton was on a cold February night and it was a bit nippy and he thought that rather than rubbing Deep Heat on to his knees, pulling his socks up over them would be a better way to keep them warm while Ivan Campo was trying to kick lumps out of him. Or maybe he started doing it because he is a fancy dan striker, and they always like to draw attention to themselves, don't they? Or maybe he started doing it because he is

French. Though, admittedly, that is a slightly broad generalization. There is no evidence to support my claim either, bar Eric Cantona and the Moulin Rouge.

The Moulin Rouge in Paris is where you go to watch girls dance. It is not one of those places where they pass a pint pot round afterwards. though. This is sophisticated. There are sumptuous sets, shimmering colours, live musicians and more sequins than on a Graham Norton jacket. The costumes are designer but the girls do like to show a bit of a leg and are quite often stocking-clad, which again brings us back to the tantalizing bit of flesh on show.

Eric Cantona is at the opposite end of the spectrum to the Moulin Rouge, yet he always adapted his kit to draw a bit of attention to himself. Not for him the socks-over-the-knees look, oh no. Eric was all about the upturned collar. Now, unless you were in *Grease* or you were a European male over the age of twenty-five who also wore a jumper over your shoulders, you didn't put your collar up. Ever. Eric did. It gave him a regal air. It added to the sense that he was at a level above everybody else and made you notice him even more. Was Thierry Henry looking to give himself a similarly elitist aura?

It would make sense. He was one of the greatest footballers to have ever played in the Premier League. He had speed and skill like very few others so your eyes were always drawn to his feet and his legs, and then you would notice that he wore his socks differently to everybody else. That isn't the case any more? Every Tom, Dick and Harry, or rather Cristiano, Fernando and JT, wears them this way now.

Yet Henry, Ronaldo or Torres wearing his socks in this way doesn't really bother me. They are European, exotic and skilful. The slightly effeminate way of wearing their socks tends to suit them. But if you are a 'lion-heart' then the look really isn't for you.

The amateur side that I play for has one of these 'lion-hearts'. He is a central midfielder from Hull, a policeman who now lives in London. He is 6'3", and at a guess I would say fourteen stone. I have never seen him lose a header. Opposition players bounce off him. He likes a tackle and probably gets a couple of red cards a season. However, in the past couple of seasons he has started to wear his socks over his knees. Or at least he does at the start of the season. Post-Christmas, after most of the team have washed the kit at the wrong temperature or tumble-dried it hot, you are lucky if you can get the socks halfway up your legs and over your shin pads. My team-mate starts the season trying to look like Thierry Henry and ends it with a passing resemblance to Juan Sebastian Verón.

Verón cost £28 million when Alex Ferguson signed him for Manchester United, and the only memory he provided me with was how he wore his socks. Money well spent, Fergie. He obviously didn't like wearing his socks up but he had to wear shin pads, so he carefully folded his socks around his pads. It must have taken some planning in the dressing room beforehand. He must have spent so much time perfecting the look that he didn't pay any attention to the team talks, and thus was crap. Still, at least he wasn't Eric Djemba-Djemba. I have no idea how he wore his socks.

The 'lion-hearts' of years gone by had their socks as far from their thighs as they possibly could. If you were a hard-man in the seventies and eighties, your toughness was partly gauged on how low down your legs you could roll your socks. Any centre-half worth his salt would have his socks round his ankles. Shin pads were for players who were scared of getting hurt. Now, of course, for insurance purposes and because a broken leg really isn't very nice and tends to smart quite a bit, shin pads have to be worn and socks have to cover them.

So, JT, if you had played thirty years ago you would have worn your socks round your ankles, I am sure of it. Nowadays you can't. But just have a word with yourself, will you? You are as tough as old boots, and you like to cultivate that image. So please, stop wearing your socks in a girly, semi-erotic way.

Still, at least you don't wear the most effeminate garment available to modern footballers.

Hairbands

Nob is a word that has cropped up already in this book, and if you actually manage to get to the end of the whole thing then you will firstly have my gratitude and admiration, but secondly you will notice that it is a word I use an awful lot.

This is partly because it is one of my favourite words, but also because it does apply to an awful lot of people connected to the beautiful game. Yes, it is a term of abuse, but in a slightly endearing way. It is nowhere near as harsh as some other expletives which, if I mentioned them here, would be gratuitous and just a way to get closer to the number of words I have agreed with my publishers. So when I call somebody a nob I am not doing it with malice or hatred, I am doing it out of annoyance, with just a small amount of affection thrown in. I find that the word 'tit' can perform a similar function.

And so it was on 15 July 2009 I was watching a Carlos Tevez press conference while mouthing 'nob' over and over again at the television screen. The little Argentine striker was sat alongside Mark Hughes as he was presented to the media as a Manchester City striker. As a supporter of the red half of the city, you would assume that was the reason for my use of obscenities. But you would have been completely wrong. He may have wronged my club, he may have been a terrace favourite who had crossed the divide, he may even have made some disparaging comments about Sir Alex Ferguson, but all of that paled into insignificance compared to the quite ridiculous garment he had on his head.

With sponsors' boards behind him and the world's media's microphones in front, there were plenty of things my eyes could have been drawn to, yet they were fixed on a huge white headband that was pushing back his silky black locks. I can't tell you what it was made of – it looked like it was woollen (but that would be a ridiculous material to wear in the height of summer, even a British summer) – but I can tell you what it made him look like. A nob.

Tevez had played two seasons for Manchester United in some kind of loan deal that was far too complicated to understand. His industry and work rate turned him into a favourite with the Stretford End. He wasn't the most prolific of scorers, but fans love a trier, don't they? Northern fans – and whatever people may say, most of them inside Old Trafford are northern and from Manchester – also don't like fancy dans. They want their heroes to be strong, fierce and intimidating. They don't want posers and preeners and players who look immaculately groomed. And United fans are no different. Keane, Cantona and Robson evoke more affection in the hearts of the Red Army than Ronaldo.

This makes the taking to the bosom of Tevez even more

remarkable. True, he isn't blessed with stunning good looks – it could even be said that he banged into a few branches on his way down the ugly tree – but he did wear a headband. Northern men don't do headbands. If you are from north of Birmingham and your hair is starting to get too long you don't use a hairband to keep it out of your eyes. Instead, you go and see your mam, she gets out one of her bowls, puts it over your bonce, and cuts off any hair left poking out. And if you are a non-believer, or southern, then I offer as evidence Ian Brown, Mani, the Inspiral Carpets and the Gallagher brothers.

In Tevez's defence, it could be argued that his hairband was black so not nearly as visible as the white monstrosity he chose to wear at his City unveiling, and also that it was chunky and quite manly, in so far as such a garment can be described as manly. Dimitar Berbatov has no such defence.

The languid 6'2" Bulgarian arrived at Manchester United the season after Tevez. He hasn't reached fans' favourite status. Worryingly, he hasn't reached any status with the fans. He is not hated or despised or loved or adored. There is a kind of indifference towards him. Before Tevez departed, pundits speculated on why Tevez was the popular one out of the two of them. The easy, and lazy, theory that was universally agreed on was that it was because Tevez ran and harried whereas Berbatov strolled and lolloped. They ignored the fact that Tevez wore a chunky hairband whereas Berbatov wore something out of your fourteen-year-old sister's jewellery box. Tevez was the more popular one because he looked slightly less ridiculous.

Since arriving in this country from Bayer Leverkusen, Berbatov has always worn this thin black stringy hairband, both at Tottenham Hotspur and United. If he had a long, flowing mane it would be easier to excuse, but he doesn't. His hair always seems lank and plastered to his head with water or gel. It doesn't even get close to getting in his eyes, thereby affecting his vision. Yet he has to tie it back with this very feminine hair accessory. All it does is highlight that he has a massive forehead.

I was born in the seventies but don't really remember watching football until the eighties. My only knowledge of football pre-1980 comes from watching a lot of ESPN Classic. The seventies saw a lot of footballers, most footballers, with long hair. The majority of games look like matches between Bee Gees tribute acts. Yet there is not a hairband to be seen. George Best weaves through defences with his hair blowing in the wind, Charlie George celebrates a winning FA Cup Final goal with socks rolled down and hair everywhere, Kevin Keegan chins Billy Bremner through a mop of curls and jet black fury, and Bobby Charlton just kept combing over the same four strands. Hairbands were for other sports, like John McEnroe in tennis or the fat ones in rugby union scrums, to pin back their funny-shaped ears. They weren't for football.

Brighton and Hove Albion's Steve Foster has the honour of being the first player I remember seeing in a hairband (although he could argue it was more of a sweatband than a haircare product). Over and above Ray Wilkins' curler or Gary Bailey saving from Gordon Smith, his white towelling band is my stand-out image of the 1983 FA Cup Final. With such interests, it could easily have been Toni and Mark for me. They were rare back then though – hairbands on footballers, not hairdressers – which is why I suppose I noticed them. Now, though, at the risk of sounding like the *Daily Mail* talking about Eastern European immigrants, they are everywhere. Chris Eagles at Burnley is another with a stringy Berbatov-style hairband. At Burnley, I ask you. It should be about pints and pies and bracing winds on a rainy Tuesday night at Turf Moor whenever you talk about the club. Poncy hairbands have no place in stereotypical northern settings.

So if you are a player and you're thinking about wearing a hairband, please just cut your hair and save yourself the ridicule, or join a club in that there fancy cosmopolitan London.

Boots

DJ Spoony (I am such a name-dropper, I know) walked into the changing rooms at Upton Park with a massive cardboard box in his arms. 'It's OK, lads,' he bellowed, 'I have sorted the boots out for today. I have got you all a pair.'

We were about to play in the Celebrity Soccer Six tournament at West Ham, an all-day-long, six-a-side tournament that features celebrities. In the build-up to it, the public and those of us playing are often told that Ant 'n' Dec will be there, or Take That, or Sienna Miller. You then end up playing against Sam 'n' Mark, Goldie Lookin' Chain and some bird who got into the final seven of *Big Brother 5*.

Spoony made sure that we were all dressed in the home team's changing room before we were allowed to delve into the box. Once we had on our black socks, black shorts and black and white shirts, me, Lee Sharpe, Colin Murray, DJ Sammy and Tinhead from *Brookside* all gathered round the box. I love getting new boots. The feel of them, the smell of them, the fact that they are clean and not caked in mud. My fellow footballing luminaries felt the same, apart from

Sharpe, for whom this was just going to be another set of boots. When you are a pro and you get a new pair for every single game, it probably isn't that exciting getting some off an R&B DJ while stood next to the bloke who remixed Bryan Adams' 'Heaven'.

The box was opened and I took out a smaller box that indicated there were a pair of size 10s within. What wasn't indicated was that the boots inside were white.

White!

Spoony had got his hands on a job lot of white boots.

Alan Ball was the first person to wear white boots as the sixties turned into the seventies. 'I remember thinking he must have been some player to wear those white boots,' said David O'Leary, 'and Alan Ball *was* some player.' And therein was my problem. Alan Ball was some player and could get away with whatever colour boots he wanted. I wasn't some player, and my technical limitations were about to be shown up in bright white shiny boots.

I wished I had brought my own pair to the tournament, because I have never ever worn anything other than a pair of black boots. I have tried different manufacturers over the years, switched between studs and blades, and even believed the bollocks – sorry, science about some boots swerving the ball better than others. However, when I wore a pair of those I seemed to slice the ball into touch more often than before. I blamed the new swerve technology on my feet, rather than a lack of ability. Not one pair of boots has ever helped the problem of my first touch leading to my second touch being a lunging tackle.

Of course now I can take my pick of boot colour. There isn't a colour invented that hasn't been painted on to a football boot. Ben, and his team-mates, want any colour other than black. They don't see their heroes in black boots, only their ageing cumbersome dads when they come to watch us play, so for them the boots have to be orange or red or blue or whatever colour Ronaldo, Lampard or Fabregas wore last weekend.

Colours is one thing, but the ridiculous thing that has crept into, or rather on to, the boots over the past few years is identification. I can't be sure about where this craze started or who it started with but I am willing to bet a few quid that it is David Beckham's fault. He was the first footballer I can remember having his shirt number and his initials stitched into his boots. It was his mother's idea to do this.

After every game, he would come home with someone else's boots. Gary Neville's one week, Ole Gunnar Solskjaer's the next. When he turfed Jaap Stam's massive footwear out of his kit bag, Mrs Beckham decided enough was enough. She couldn't stitch a name tag on to his boots, like she used to with his school jumper, so instead she phoned up Adidas and asked if there was any way they could tag his boots. I mean tag in an identification kind of way, not in a Jermaine Pennant kind of way. And lo and behold they came up with sticking his squad number and his initials on the heel of the boot, or on the tongue, or in some cases on both.

Once Beckham had it, they all wanted it. Now you are not on the A-list of footballers unless you have something written on your boots. This can be your squad number, your name, your nickname or the names of family members (children are the favourite ones to put on for the simple reason they will never change because they will always be your kids. It's advisable not to put your other half's name on your boots because you never know when you might ditch her for a younger, fitter model, or get caught in a threesome in a hotel suite by the *News of the World*). You can even have the flag of the country of your birth, or the flag of the country you play for, if that is different, on your boots. If you are a Premier League player and you don't have this nonsense all over your footwear then your boot manufacturers don't really care that much about you. You aren't one of their top stars.

Yet this service is available to amateur players. I know this because I recently bought some new sensible black boots, with screw-in studs, and was offered the chance to personalize them. It would have cost me quite a bit more money to have 'Chapman 6' added to the heel of each boot, and it would have meant a whole season of mickey-taking from my team-mates, so I declined. I also know this because I now come up against amateur players on a Saturday afternoon who, rather than 'Brooklyn' and 'Romeo', are running around with 'Chanel' and 'Jackson' on their boots. Beckham 7 is replaced by the likes of Smith 25, which I can only assume is their weight in stone because we don't have squad numbers at our level but we do have fat bastards.

It might be embarrassing for big lumps my age to be messing about with all these things, but it is a nightmare for the kids. Too much choice can be a bad thing. When I was playing at school and in youth football, the only thing that concerned me was whether the studs were metal. It was a bonus if they were because I could then sharpen them on the concrete path that led to the pitches. I wasn't a very nice child. Now kids have too much to worry about. Manufacturer, colour, studs or blades, a message to put on them – it can all damage their street cred. Ben's little boots are the right side of cool, apparently. Do you think me getting 'Daddy 6' or 'Daddy is great' embroidered on them would increase his street cred?

No, me neither.

THE
PLAYER

Footballers

We all know somebody who claims they had a trial at a football club when they were younger. Indeed, as you get older, there appear to be more and more people of your age group who reckon they were on the books of a football club when they were a kid. Why? Because we all wish we had been a footballer.

When you are in your teens, you feel that you could be spotted at any time and that the next game could be the one when Manchester United offer you a few weeks with the club so they can take a better look at you. Into your early twenties, you still think there is a chance but it might have to be Stockport County who see you in a game and take a punt on you. By the time the late twenties come round, you are just hopeful of anybody connected with the game seeing you running around on a Sunday morning. Into your thirties, although you aren't giving up hope, you can see that it is looking less likely, so to keep the dream alive in your head you claim you once had a trial at a football club when you were younger, or that you spent one summer on the books of a club. We just can't deal with going through the whole of our lives without having been a footballer.

I was never spotted, never had a trial, never even came close to having a trial. My only 'playing' claim-to-fame story is that Ryan Giggs played for another side in our Sunday league and I played against him a couple of times. It wouldn't surprise me if he was actually spotted while playing against our side because I made his not inconsiderable talent appear even better by being so crap.

There is a month between me and Giggs, age-wise, and while he continues to perform at the highest level, I still agree to take part in so-called 'celebrity' matches in the hope that I can still make it, or at the very least feel like a proper footballer for a while.

I have never felt more crushing disappointment than when Graham Taylor didn't pick me to be part of his squad for *The Match* on Sky One. The programme took a group of supposedly well-known people and trained them for a week before they had a match against a squad of ex-pros in front of a full house at St James's Park. I thought I had done quite well in the trial game, but men ten years older were outperforming me in fitness tests, so I was out.

A year after that, Sky changed the format, which was a relief because it meant I got a game. It turned into the Premier League All Stars, and I played for Manchester United in a tournament against the other nineteen Premier League teams at the time. We were in full United kit, with our names on the back. This was my dream, this was my moment. It might have been five-a-side on a blue and red carpet in a warehouse in East London, but I was representing Manchester United.

Our quarter-final game was against Manchester City. I was awful, as I had been in every game we played. The match ended in a draw and it went down to a penalty shoot-out. The shoot-out went down to sudden death. City were going first. They missed. It was down to me. Score, and I would put my team, Manchester United, into the semi-finals.

I strode forward. This was proper football. It didn't matter that the man in the blue shirt returning to his players after missing was the snooker player Nigel Bond, he was a Manchester City footballer in my head. And I was Bryan Robson.

I think I did every cliché going. I kissed the ball. I put it on the spot, the bright red spot on a blue carpet. I walked away with my back to the goal, thinking the keeper mustn't see my eyes. He must not be able to read which way I was going to go. I took a deep breath and wiped my sweat-drenched hands on the bottom of my red shirt. This wasn't a pissy Z-list celeb fest in a warehouse. This was Old Trafford on a dark wet windswept night in March with an FA Cup semi-final at stake.

I turned, took two steps (because you weren't allowed any more because it was a five-a-side tournament), and slammed the ball into the top corner. I went mad. I went absolutely ape shit. I ran towards the presenting booth where Jason McAteer was sat. The ex-Liverpool player had been giving me a bit of 'banter' during the game. I gave him some 'banter' back before being jumped on by Clayton Blackmore,

Angus Deayton, Lee Sharpe and Darren Campbell.

I was a Manchester United footballer.

I was buzzing. It was a high that is very difficult to put into words. Under a burning hot shower afterwards I felt such contentment, I felt such pleasure with the laughter and jokes of team-mates around me, I felt like a hero, I felt delirious, I felt like an integral part of our team (which I definitely wasn't), and I felt lucky. Lucky to have had the opportunity to do what I had just done. Every single one of those feelings is something that a modern-day player feels. Well, maybe not every single feeling. I do wonder if many of them genuinely feel lucky to do what they do.

Do you see joy among players nowadays? Do you see smiles and laughter? Very rarely. I know that football is a serious business with millions of pounds at stake, but it should still be fun. It is difficult to get to know the modern-day player because his world is so different, and also because he is always on his guard. As players earn more and become more famous they become less trusting, less willing to allow people into their world or even come back into the world they have left behind.

'The world they have left behind' implies that they have died, which they haven't, of course. The world they have left behind is the one where you don't spend fifty grand on champagne in a night, where you aren't surrounded by glamour models, where you don't end up in the *News of the World*, and where you don't have your initials in ornate letters on the front gates of your house.

The House

Oh Phil. Oh Phil Phil Phil. What were you thinking? You're from Bury, lad. Your brother is the shop steward at Manchester United and you have a reputation as one of football's good blokes. You speak a lot of sense, you are hard-working, you are a footballer's footballer, and the fans of the clubs you have played for respect your hard work and one hundred per cent attitude. So, given your humility and the fact that you appear to be playing the game for love and for medals rather than money, how on earth, Philip Neville, did you end up owning the archetypal footballer's house?

Phil Neville's house was probably the best-known footballer's house in the country, on account of the fact that he did the slightly stupid thing of allowing the cameras into it. He was trying to sell Sunnyside House at the time, so allowing photos of his home to be published generated publicity that it was on the market. At the same time it allowed the world and his wife to take the piss.

There is no accounting for taste and I am not going to

criticize the Nevilles for appearing to model this house on one of Saddam Hussein's palaces. Each to their own. I am sure Linda Barker would have a field day with my minimalist grey sofa and curtains lounge combo and would probably prefer the ornate golden touches of Saddam chic applied to an eighteenth-century mansion in Lancashire.

There were photographs of nearly every room in the house all over the media when the house was put on the market back in 2008, and you won't be disappointed to learn that there was both a games room and a bar. These appear to be two staples of a football player's gaff. Until magazines started doing deals with players to have a look round their houses, the only people I knew with a bar in their house were Jack and Vera Duckworth, and despite my devotion to and obsession with *Coronation Street* I am frequently reminded that they aren't real people. Whereas the Duckworths' bar was basically a semi-circular piece of Perspex on which were balanced some crème de menthe, Tia Maria and gin, with a shelf underneath, the bars in these mansions are slightly bigger. They occupy a whole room, invariably decked out in mahogany, and with a variety of pub game machines in the corner.

Two things have always bothered me about this set-up. The first is this: if you go round to their houses and play the machines, do you have to put money in them? And if so, do these multi-millionaires on eighty grand a week keep the proceeds? The second thing is, why do they always try to re-create a ye olde worlde country pub in their houses? I don't see many footballers frequenting such establishments. I can't remember the last time I saw a player eating his chicken in a basket while supping on a pint of mild and playing dominoes with his companion. Surely they should be re-creating 'The Dining Room' or 'Candy Lounge' or 'Mooaharaki' or any number of the ridiculously named bars they frequent. The room shouldn't be mahogany clad, it should be all steel, glass and smoke. Instead of pub quiz machines in the corner there could just be a gaggle of coke-addled slappers, and the money they lost by not having the machines could be recouped by charging fifty quid per glass of champagne or vodka, although that might be on the cheap side. If they wanted to make it even more authentic, I'm sure they could afford somebody to stand in their bog for a couple of hours a night handing out lollipops and moisturizer. The quiz machines could then go into the games room, along with the snooker table or the pool table, the table football, the air hockey and the massive flatscreen telly connected to a Wii, a PS3 and Xbox, because why have one format when you can have all three?

Most footballers will then have this room leading on to the indoor swimming pool. The indoor swimming pool is always quite a good indication of where the modern player is in his life or his career. How can you tell this? Because of the mosaic at the bottom of the pool.

They all have to have a mosaic. If the mosaic is of the club crest then he is likely to be playing for that club for a while to come. I have no knowledge of the pool industry but I imagine that mosaics are a bugger to change, and expensive too. So, unless a clause is inserted in a transfer that the buying club has to pay for the player's new swimming pool mosaic, he is going to be staying put for a while. If the design on the bottom is of the player's wife or children, then he is the kind of settled family man that managers like to have at their clubs. When managers talk about doing research into a player's background to find out how suitable he is for their club, they are often talking about researching the swimming pool history of the player first and foremost. If the player has chosen a mosaic of himself then he is an egotistical nob and best avoided.

Lining the walls of the games room, no matter which footballer's house you are in, are framed signed shirts. These will be a mix of a player's own shirts from big games and shirts from opponents he has swapped with. It is fascinating to have a look at the shirts to see who players have swapped with. In one of the photos of Phil Neville's games room there is a framed Juventus shirt. It has on the back of it the number 14 and the name Deschamps. Didier Deschamps also played for Marseille and Chelsea and was the youngest captain to lead his side to the Champions League title, as well, of course, as being the man who captained France to the World Cup in his homeland in 1998. Do you think he has Phil Neville's shirt framed and hanging on the wall in his games room in the south of France?

The trophies and the medals that a footballer has won don't tend to be on display. They are usually kept in a bank vault, I am led to believe, because they are valuable. Mind you, framed signed shirts are not to be sniffed at. I was once sent a Manchester United shirt with 'Chappers 1' on the back. I decided to take it to a David Beckham interview and asked him to sign it, which he did. I then thought that would make a great Christmas present for my mum and dad. I have no idea why, because my mum couldn't really care less about David Beckham and has always called me Mark. It was a massively egotistical thing to do, and it was a massively expensive thing to do: I thought I was getting away with a cheapy pressie for them, but it ended up costing around £150 to frame the bloody thing. Footballers seem to have at least twenty framed shirts each, and given that they have all been worn by some world-class players and have cost £150 a time to frame, they are worth a few bob.

So, given that footballers have a lot of expensive gear in their houses, from shirts to technology to jewellery, it would seem a little daft to advertise who lives there. It seems even dafter when you consider that over the last eighteen months there has been a spate of burglaries in the north-west of England where the properties of footballers have been broken into while the players were playing away. (By that I mean actually playing a match somewhere, not nobbing a glamour model.) So if you were a footballer, you would spend thousands getting your security system up to scratch to protect yourself and your property, wouldn't you? No, you wouldn't. What you would actually do is spend thousands of pounds getting your initial and that of your partner engraved, in beautifully ornate lettering, on the gates of your property. That's what Phil and his missus did. The gates of their house were decorated with a massive P and a massive J (she's called Julie).

Property experts believe they struggled to sell the house for a long time because of the collapse of the market and the recession. In fact it was because you had to have the initials P and J in the family to be able to buy it. Otherwise a massive redecorating bill would come attached to the place. Because not only were Phil and Julie's initials on the gate, they were all over the house. On the curtains and stitched into the deep shagpile carpets, among other places. It was as if they needed a reminder of who they were every now and then. 'What you called again, love? Oh yeah, it's Julie, isn't it? I've just seen it on the shagpile.'

Posh and Becks did something similar when they bought their massive country mansion. It was called Beckingham Palace (see what they did there? Very clever). According to reports, when you first went through the front door you were confronted by a massive black and white photo of the happy couple canoodling, as my gran would say. Did they sometimes forget who they were coming home to? Did their visitors arrive and then suddenly forget who it was they were dropping in on? Or did they just want to make sure that they could never appear on *Through the Keyhole*? Probably none of those. It was probably a nice photo and an ego thing. Footballers like having stuff to do with themselves up around their houses because they themselves are their favourite subjects.

Our elite footballers like to separate themselves from the rest of us. They don't want to be bothered by us normal fans, they want to be left in peace on their pedestals, and idolized. They don't want us to know where they live because when they close those initialled gates behind them they need to rest and have some peace. They don't want us all to know their movements when they leave their houses so they don't get pestered for autographs as they leave their pimped-up Baby Bentleys in team colours with personalized number plates in a disabled parking space because they can't be arsed to walk an extra fifty yards and can afford the fine. And they don't want to be photographed on a night out when they leave the most talked-about city centre club with two Day-Glo models on their arm and with the bloke who plays a street sweeper in *EastEnders* trailing behind them. No, they most definitely don't want any of that. They want their football to do the talking, not their houses, not their cars, and most definitely not their missus.

WAGs

When England went out of the 2006 World Cup in Germany, they were beaten on penalties by Portugal. They had been reduced to ten men during normal time when Wayne Rooney stamped on Ricardo Carvalho's knackers. Cristiano Ronaldo urged the referee to show a red card, and when the official did so, he winked towards Luis Felipe Scolari and the rest of the Portuguese bench. Ronaldo became public enemy number one and most of the blame for England's elimination was laid at his door. The rest of it wasn't apportioned to the England players, Sven-Göran Eriksson, the inability to score from twelve yards or Rooney for his impetuous stupidity. It was instead blamed on the wives and girlfriends of the England team who had been out in Germany for the tournament and had kept the media busy by going on shopping trips several times a day.

They were a group of women who travelled out to watch their other halves take part in the biggest tournament of their lives. They were there to support them, to cheer them and, if they had children, to take the kids to watch Daddy in the World Cup. They were a support to the players. Yet they also had time to kill. And this may seem stereotypical, but they did that in the two best ways women know how: shopping and getting pampered. It wasn't their fault that their presence turned into a media circus. It wasn't their fault that when they went out the media ended up on their tail, cameras snapping perpetually in a blaze of fake tans and hair extensions.

Victoria Beckham and Cheryl Cole sat together at that tournament. The two highest-profile WAGs, held up as bad examples of this new breed of women with famous footballing other halves. Except, of course, they had their own careers before they met their husbands. The Spice Girls and Girls Aloud were quite successful in their own right. Most of the WAGs do have careers, and if they aren't working professionally then they are looking after the children.

If it wasn't for the WAGs, a lot of our footballers would be way off the straight and narrow. The WAGs do their best to keep them in check: they stop them thinking about themselves all the time and they give them some perspective. It is no surprise that managers want as many of their players married off and with kids as soon as possible. It keeps them stable.

The problem is, the WAGs get lumped in with the kiss-and-tells and the serial shaggers, those girls who move from one player to another, each time getting more press coverage, getting more orange and getting a new pair of tits. They are the ones who should be getting the stick in the press, but they hardly ever do because they are normally 'glamour' girls who the papers employ. There are girls out there who have been through nearly a whole dressing room. That can't do a lot for team morale, can it? If several players in the team I supported had all been with the same girl, then I would worry about what was being talked about in the changing room. I would worry that jealousy might creep into the squad – an 'I'm not passing to him because Chantelle said he was better in bed than me' attitude – and I would certainly be avoiding jumping in the team bath if I was one of their team-mates.

WAGs tend to keep their counsel, unlike the serial shaggers, who are in the papers every day with the secrets of the footballers. I honestly don't care about the size of a certain player's tackle (because they always have to do the puns, don't they?), or how he certainly knew what he was doing in the box, or that he is an accomplished defender because he had her two impressive strikers under control. However, I know this because I read about it. So maybe if we all stopped reading the kiss-and-tells, the papers would stop publishing them, the serial slappers wouldn't be able to sell them, and the WAGs wouldn't get lumped in with these types of girls and would instead get a bit of the respect they deserve.

Not full respect though, because they are still far too orange.

Autobiographies

In 2008, Joey Barton managed the not inconsiderable feat of being done for assault twice within a six-week period. In the May of that year he was imprisoned for an attack that left a teenage boy with shattered teeth. The judge described it as a 'violent and cowardly attack'. While in jail for that attack, Barton received a four-month suspended sentence for battering his former Manchester City team-mate Ousmane Dabo. The French midfielder ended up in hospital with facial injuries and a suspected detached retina. Throw in that Barton was once sent home from a pre-season tour in Thailand for attacking a teenage Everton supporter in the hotel reception, and that at a Manchester City Christmas party he stubbed out a cigar in a reserve goalkeeper's eye, and you have somebody who isn't one of the nicest or one of the most popular characters in the game.

Yet Joey Barton has come up with one of the most memorable quotes from any player over the past ten years. 'England did nothing in that World Cup, so why were they bringing books out? "We got beat in the quarter-final. I played like shit. Here's my book." '

It could very well be one of my favourite quotes of all time. Barton didn't care that he was criticizing fellow professionals or that he could very well end up playing alongside them in the future, he was just saying what we were all thinking as Steven Gerrard, Frank Lampard, Rio Ferdinand and Ashley Cole all brought out autobiographies after that 2006 World Cup defeat to Portugal. What on earth did they all have to write about?

I have no idea because I haven't read any of them. I would imagine they included the World Cup quarter-final that Barton referred to, although I imagine their wording would be different. I am assuming they all had a bit on their childhood, followed by loads and loads of stuff on how great it is to be a footballer and win trophies, while at the same time trying to give the impression of just being normal blokes. That is, all except Ashley Cole, who can't give the impression of being a normal bloke because his book, *My Defence*, included this memorable quote: 'When I heard Jonathan [Cole's agent] repeat the figure of £55k, I nearly swerved off the road. "He is taking the piss, Jonathan!" I yelled down the phone. I was so incensed.' He nearly crashed his car because Arsenal's new contract offer was £55,000 a week. If somebody offered me £55,000 a week I would nearly swerve off the road as well, but in shock not anger. Cole had wanted £60,000 a week. I would advocate it wasn't the best thing for Cole to put in his book, as it made him sound like a money-grabbing tosser. But he was only twenty-five at the time, and he had a lot of pages to fill, so he had to put everything in.

They were all in their mid to late twenties when these books came out. Why didn't they all wait until their careers were over and they had more to write about and more life experiences? Oh yeah, because they wanted to cash in, that's why. Wayne Rooney also brought a book out after the World Cup. It was his first in a twelve-year five-book deal with his publishers that is worth around £5 million. He is going to have to achieve a heck of a lot over the rest of his career to make each one of them worth reading. I am assuming there will be quite a few photographs in them.

I am thinking that criticizing other people's books in a book of your own might not be the best thing to do – people in glass houses, and all that – and at this stage of reading mine, you could well be thinking, 'Why didn't I pick up the book next to this on the shelf? Surely *Theo Walcott – My Life up to the Age of 14* would have been a better read than this?' His would have more photographs, certainly. When I told people I was writing a book, they all asked if it was an autobiography. Why would I write an autobiography? I am not well known, I haven't achieved anything and I'm under forty. These are the criteria for a sporting autobiography, and most footballers only satisfy the first one.

All of the footballers mentioned above could have waited until they had finished their careers before writing their memoirs, and I would have read every single one of them. They could have been thoughtful, retrospective and meaningful. They would have been able to put their careers into perspective and the writing would certainly have been more mature.

People will buy and read sporting autobiographies whenever they are released if they are good and the person has a story to tell. Rushing books out in the hope of riding the crest of a wave of a World Cup victory is a dangerous gamble, mainly because we have only ever won one of the blooming things, and it's an insult to our intelligence as fans. Riding the crest of a penalties defeat to Portugal didn't really work as well as if we had won the tournament, so nobody cashed in as much as they had hoped.

Did the players really need the money? Was it really worth them opening themselves up to ridicule from upstanding members of the footballing community such as Joey Barton? The answer to both is no. But so long as the players are surrounded by people with so many different interests, agents, publishers, literary agents and PR people who can all make money out of them, then they will be pressured into delivering whatever is asked of them.

I, on the other hand, do need the money, so if you are liking it so far then please tell as many people as possible about it and suggest they buy a copy. Don't offer to lend them the one you are reading, because that doesn't benefit anybody. And if you aren't enjoying it so far, then there is plenty to come, I promise. I talk about Graham Poll later so that's got to be worth you sticking with it. Unless the very mention of his name makes you want to swerve off the road in anger.

Squad Numbers

The number 10 shirt is the most romantic in world football. No matter what the team, be it club or country, it is seen as the symbol of the beautiful game. It has been worn by some of the sport's greatest players: Pelé, Maradona, Puskas, Platini, Baggio, Bergkamp, Zidane and Gallas have all plied their trade with 10 on their backs.

Can you spot the odd one out? What the bloody hell is William Gallas doing wearing 10?

Personally, I have nothing against Gallas. He is a superb French international defender who, despite having the personality of a moody toddler, can play anywhere across the back four. He has captained Arsenal, and formed a decent central defensive partnership with Kolo Touré, and now Thomas Vermaelen. Yes, he's a cultured centre-half, not a big tough lump, but even so, he should never be wearing the number 10 shirt. Touré wore the traditional shirt for a centre-half, 5. Vermaelen took over that number. Good men.

Squad numbers have been regularly used in English club football since 1993, brought in as a clever money-making device. Every player would have his name on the back of his shirt, above a number that he would keep for the whole of that season. Therefore if you wanted to be like your hero, you could buy your replica shirt and for an extra few quid have his name and number ironed on to the back of it. Unfortunately, the other thing that the introduction of squad numbers did was turn those of us who were already quite anal about these kinds of things into complete obsessives.

There are three people who I feel should take most of the blame for my unhealthy interest in this subject: Ron Greenwood, Lee Sharpe and Milan Baros.

Greenwood was the England manager for the 1982 World Cup in Spain. It is the first World Cup I can remember, and at that time major international football tournaments were the only matches when squad numbers were used. It was quite exciting when the squad was announced to see who had been allocated which number (Playstations hadn't been invented then, so we had to make our own entertainment). But Greenwood went and ruined it. He gave the goalkeepers their usual numbers (Ray Clemence 1, Joe Corrigan 13 and Peter Shilton 22, in case you are interested), and then gave the number 7 shirt to his captain, Kevin Keegan. The others he allocated in alphabetical order. That was how my school did everything. Surely the England manager could be more imaginative? There I was, an eight-year-old boy, wondering whether Trevor Brooking or Glenn Hoddle would get the coveted number 10, or whether Paul Mariner or Tony Woodcock would get the number 9, when in fact Greenwood was doing a decent impression of Mrs Barnes allocating the coat pegs for my class cloakroom. As I am sure you are dying to know, Brooking wore 3, Hoddle 9, Mariner 11 and Woodcock 21. Pure madness.

In future tournaments, England allocated the numbers slightly more sensibly, and of course some shirt numbers have become iconic. Paul Gascoigne's number 19 from the tear-ravaged 1990 World Cup semi-final remains a popular retro shirt for England fans.

At this point, you're probably thinking, 'How on earth did this man ever get a girlfriend, let alone eventually persuade a woman to marry him and have his child?' And maybe also, 'I bet he was a bit too excited when the Premier League introduced squad numbers.' And you'd be right. About both of them.

I remember looking at my own club's first list of squad numbers and being disappointed by two things. Firstly, my beloved Bryan Robson had not been given the number 7 shirt that he had worn with distinction for many years. He had been asked to wear 12. (The 7 went to Eric Cantona, so at least he was equally deserving.) But the oddest choice was that Lee Sharpe had been given the number 5. He was a left-winger, as well as being an Elvis impersonator – the perfect number 11 – so why had he been given a centre-half's number?

The number 5 seems to be unfairly treated with disregard by some club managers. When Milan Baros joined Liverpool in 2002, he was also given that number. Baros was a striker – admittedly a striker who had the scoring rate of a centre-half, but all the same.

Now, since Sharpe and Baros, every single ridiculous and inappropriate squad number really catches my eye. Spurs gave Paul Stalteri the 7 shirt. He's a right-back. Arsène Wenger not only gave Gallas 10, he also made Abou Diaby number 2. He's a midfielder, not a right-back. José Mourinho was anything but special when he gave Khalid Bhoularouz the number 9. He was a defender, not a target man. Steve Finnan was Liverpool's right-back yet he wore 3, and then their left-back, Andrea Dossena, was given the number 2 shirt. That's the wrong way round.

Most players would prefer to wear a number between 1 and 11, but that can't be the case in these days of ever-expanding squads, so shirt numbers are getting bigger and bigger. There are normally three reasons why players wear a shirt number larger than 20. Firstly, they are young players who have just broken into the first-team squad, and in the cases of John Terry (26), Jamie Carragher (23) and Sol Campbell (23), they decided to keep those original numbers. Secondly, a player signs in the January transfer window and there are no small numbers spare. Thirdly, they are shit, are hardly going to get a game, and therefore nobody notices they've been given 43.

Certain numbers do have special significance at clubs. The number 7 shirt is *the* shirt at both Liverpool and Manchester United. This started at Anfield in the 1970s when it was worn by both Kevin Keegan and Kenny Dalglish. Peter Beardsley took on the mantle in the 1980s, and if we gloss over Vladimir Smicer and Harry Kewell's contributions, it was then passed on to Robbie Keane. Keane grew up with

Dalglish as his boyhood hero, so he was living every fan's dream. At United, the 7 shirt has been worn by Best, Coppell, Robson, Cantona, Beckham and then Cristiano Ronaldo. When Keane and Ronaldo moved on, the fans were obviously keen that the shirt was passed to somebody deserving. As I write this, Liverpool have no number 7. United's is worn by a former Liverpool striker.

Some clubs are now taking the step of retiring shirt numbers if they have been worn by a great player. This is ridiculous. Surely a great shirt number becomes legendary because of all the players that have worn it. It should not be retired. Having said that, when clubs retire shirt numbers in memory of players, you have to applaud them for the gesture. Manchester City retired their number 23 after the tragic death of Marc-Vivien Foé. The Cameroon midfielder had scored the final ever goal by a City player at their old Maine Road ground in April 2003. Barely two months later he collapsed on the pitch while representing his country. Nobody at West Ham will wear the number 6 any more in tribute to the late, great Bobby Moore.

When I present Italian football matches, you can sometimes see me squirming when I spot players wearing ridiculous numbers. Cristiano Lucarelli turned out for his hometown club, Livorno, with 99 on his back. This was in tribute to the club's Ultras group of fans, which had been founded in 1999. The goalkeeper Gianluigi Buffon picked 88 as his number for one season. This didn't go down too well as 88 is sometimes equated with the Nazi Party. H is the eighth letter of the alphabet, so 88 can stand for HH, which in turn can signify Heil Hitler. Buffon denied this was the case, and said the number 88 reminded him of four balls, and if he had four balls he would not only have three more than Hitler had but be very tough indeed. He changed to number 1 not long after.

I've now taken my numbers obsession into everyday life. As I said, I play football on a Saturday afternoon for an amateur side called Ibis. The standard isn't bad. We even have oranges at half-time. At the end of every game one lad has to take the kit home to wash. He then brings it with him the following week and the kit bag is dumped in the middle of the changing-room floor. As you arrive in the dressing room, hopefully a good hour before kick-off but usually two minutes before because the traffic was bad, the bus was late or you got hammered the night before, you delve into the bag and take out a pair of socks, some shorts and a slightly damp shirt that hasn't been dried properly. Nobody else in my team ever checks what number he is pulling out of the bag, but I ferret around for ages, always trying to find the number 6. My centre-forward doesn't care if he has the number 4 shirt, or my left-back if he is wearing 9, and the guy on the bench is putting his tracksuit top over the hallowed number 7. I think it makes us look like a joke outfit. And that's before we've started playing.

There is a huge part of me that thinks I should leave my squad number confessional right here. However, there is one more thing I have to admit to.

I play *Football Manager*. Nothing to be that ashamed of there. It is a massively popular computer game that hundreds of thousands of people play, and it really does make you feel like a proper manager. The thing with it is that before the start of each season it asks you to allocate the squad numbers to your players. I spend several hours doing this, making sure that I am happy that my squad have the correct numbers for their position and seniority. I make sure my younger players have higher numbers because they have to earn the right to wear 1 to 11. The numbers to cherish are 7 and 10, and my centre-forward always gets 9. But it's a bloody computer game. What am I doing?

My obsession does allow me, though, to dispense some advice to both fans and players when it comes to what to wear on the back of your shirt.

If you are a supporter:

- Don't try and do comedy on the back of your shirt. For example, 'WE 8' and then the name of your rival club underneath. This really isn't funny.
- If you are a grown man, don't have the name and number of a player on the back of your shirt. It makes you look sad. The golden rule is, if the player is younger than you, don't wear his shirt.
- Don't put your age on the back of your shirt. 'Dave 40' not only gives away that you are a nob. It gives away that you are a middle-aged nob.

I have suffered myself with that last one. I bought my little boy an England shirt for his fourth birthday and had 'BEN 4' put on the back. It was only when I got it home that I realized it was Steven Gerrard's shirt number. I, a Manc, had put a Scouser's shirt number, albeit his England shirt number, on my little boy's back. I felt dirty. I rarely let him wear it.

If you are a player, here is my advice to you:

- Don't wear a number that is specific to a certain position if you don't play in that position.
- If you are over twenty-five and get given a shirt number over 25, the manager doesn't want you at the club any more.
- Don't ask for the number 23 thinking you will be the next Michael Jordan and reap the commercial benefits.
- Don't stick a plus sign between two numbers if you can't get the shirt number you want. Putting a plus sign between the 1 and 8 on your number 18 shirt doesn't mean you are really wearing the number 9, it means you are a nob.
- Size isn't everything. If the number 6 shirt is taken, asking for 66 doesn't mean you are really wearing the number 6 shirt. It also means you are a nob.
- Choosing number 69 is not funny (unless you are a pubescent boy).
- If you are William Gallas, DON'T WEAR 10.

THE
GROUNDS

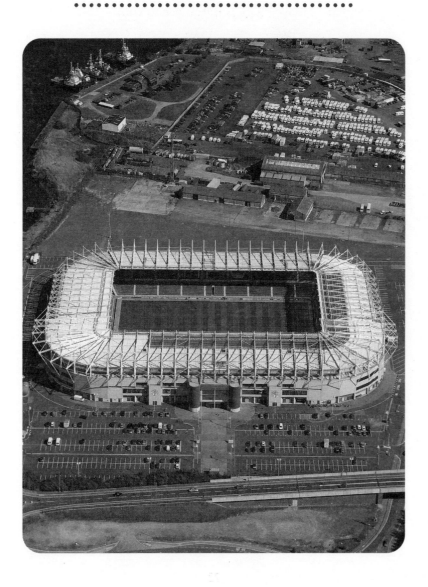

Identikit Stadia

As part of my job I have been lucky enough to cover several international football tournaments, including the European Championships in 2000 and 2004 and the World Cups of 2002 and 2006. If these competitions are highlights for a player then they should also be a highlight for a journalist or a presenter. For me they certainly were. The two World Cups still hold very fond memories for me.

The 2002 tournament was held in Japan and South Korea. I spent all my time in the former and never travelled to the latter, and had one of the most astonishing seven weeks of my life. As the world becomes smaller thanks to capitalism, big business and technology, there are fewer and fewer countries where it feels like you are abroad. Japan didn't feel like just being in another country, it felt at times like being on another planet. It was a planet that I could very happily have moved to if I felt I could have learnt the language. There was respect and courtesy everywhere, the Japanese were delighted to be hosting the tournament, and they wanted the visitors to their country to enjoy the time they were spending there. And enjoy it I did. I immersed myself in Japanese culture and loved spending time in authentic Japanese bars and restaurants. If I wasn't going to a game then an Asahi beer and a bowl of beef noodles in a little bar was the best way to watch it. It wasn't all beer and food, though. I spent a moving morning at the Kobe Port Earthquake Memorial Park. It is a tribute to the six thousand-plus people who lost their lives in the Great Hashin Quake of 1995, which measured 7.2 on the Richter scale, and the area around the Merkin Pier is conserved in its devastated condition to remind you of the horror of the disaster. Looking back, the football is a secondary memory to the country itself.

Germany in 2006 was the complete opposite. Once you have had one bratwurst you have had them all. It was all about the football and the tournament. Sweden v. England, Croatia v. Australia and Italy v. Australia were some of the more memorable games that I attended. The one that sticks in the mind, though, is Brazil v. Ghana. I was lucky enough to be sat just a couple of rows from the pitch, next to the commentator Jon Champion. It was the fastest game of football I had ever seen, the pace was unbelievable, as was the skill level, and Jon has a range of anecdotes that would make an after-dinner speaker proud. If you ever meet him, ask him to tell you about the olden-days draws for rugby league's Challenge Cup. Yet all these things were dwarfed by the experience of just being in the stadium for that match.

The Westfalenstadion in Dortmund. An immense charcoal grey and bright yellow amphitheatre of noise and passion and excitement. It was originally constructed in the early 1970s and has been upgraded and renovated over the years, the last development taking place in the run-up to the 2006 World Cup. For the game I attended there were over sixty thousand fans there, but for domestic games the ground capacity heads just north of eighty thousand. This is because when Borussia Dortmund play there, standing is still permitted; for international games, it has to be an all-seater stadium. The ground is the biggest in Germany and is dominated by *die Südtribune*, the largest free-standing grandstand in the whole of Europe, which must fascinate the architectural students among you. When Dortmund are at home, up to twenty-five thousand fans are packed on to its terraces. Even during the Brazil/Ghana game, when the fans were sitting rather than standing and therefore fewer in number, the noise and atmosphere that tumbled down from *die Südtribune* was spine-tingling.

Sat there, in the German sunshine, I felt like I was in a proper football stadium. Every stand looked different yet there was no doubt that each one was designed to make the atmosphere as special as possible. I doubt there is a stadium anywhere else in the world that is as perfect for both fans and players.

The Fritz-Walter-Stadion is on a smaller scale to the West-falenstadion. Just under fifty thousand can squeeze into the home of FC Kaiserslautern. Again, though, it was designed to create maximum noise, and the stands are a mixture of red and white designs, with both ends quite steep. The stands down the length of the pitch can feel quite old-fashioned, but there are also glass and steel towers incorporated into one of them. But it was the location of the ground that was stunning rather than the stadium itself: the Fritz-Walter-Stadion is on top of a mountain. I watched Italy beat Australia there, thanks to a very dodgy penalty decision. There was no noise for the first ten minutes of the game because all fifty thousand of us needed to get our breath back, having climbed up a three-hundred-metre hill to get in.

Knackered I may have been, but it was a lovely walk to get to the ground. Thousands of fans were climbing up winding roads with plenty of greenery to reach this citadel perched at the top. Ridiculous as it sounds, we all had a common task and a common goal. To climb and climb so that we could be rewarded with a game of football in the World Cup. It is not a feeling I have ever had walking to the Reebok.

Every stadium I went to in Germany felt different. The ground at Stuttgart was cavernous and not one of my favourites as the pitch felt remote due to being encircled by an athletics track. Frankfurt's stadium had problems with shadows, caused by a giant four-sided screen suspended over the pitch, whereas it felt quite small and intimate at Nürnberg, despite the fact that it had a forty-seven-thousand capacity and an athletics track just like Stuttgart. So, some were great and some were average, but at least there was variety.

As our older grounds in this country are knocked down or renovated, we lose variety. Our stadia are now built to the same plans. Nothing is different. If Prince Charles had an interest in the national game rather than worrying about barracks being turned into flats for posh people, he would surely have something to say about our football administrators and their architectural practices.

Is there any difference in going to the Reebok or the JJB Stadium, St Mary's or the Walkers, the KC Stadium or Pride Park? The Madejski Stadium is blue and white and the Riverside is red and white, but they are the same apart from that, aren't they? There is a uniformity within these grounds. The stands are all the same, several of them are just big bowls, and they are all a safe distance from the pitch. Fans are not right on top of the players so it is not an intimidating visit for away teams. The grounds are shallow, and by that I mean there is no steep banking like in Dortmund so the noise does not tumble down towards the pitch in cacophonous wave after cacophonous wave.

The most damning thing that you can say about most of our new stadia is that they are nice. You have a pleasant enough time when you go to any of them. You don't have an experience. Another reason for this is the location of the majority of them. No tops of mountains for these shiny new behemoths, no town-centre position with bars and restaurants near by so that fans can relax beforehand. Oh no. The only place these things are built near or in nowadays is retail parks. Soulless, huge, depressing retail parks. Perfect if you need a new carpet from Carpetworld, a dog collar from Pets R Us or a drive-thru McDonald's before you get your football fix, but not ideal if you want your matchday experience to be just that. An experience.

I had an amazing experience at the new Wembley, but as a 'player' not a spectator. I was incredibly fortunate to play in the first ever match at the stadium as part of a community day. The idea was to check that everything in the ground was working before it was opened up for 'proper' events and matches. While everybody else playing was trying to take the first kick-off at the new Wembley, the first corner or, most importantly, score the first goal (yes, Mark Bright, we know it was you), I was seeing how far I could hoof it. I managed to reach the second tier and was very proud of that.

What sticks in the mind most about that day, though, is the number of people connected with the stadium or the FA who kept asking us all what we thought of the new place. And again I come back to that word 'nice'. It was nice and pleasant and I would have expected nothing less as it cost over £800 million. Having returned several times as a spectator, and walked from Wembley Park down the barren wasteland – sorry, down Wembley Way to get there, it is still nice. And soulless, and expensive. A box of Maltesers at the 2007 Cup Final for my boy cost nearly four quid. That makes this book look like a bargain. Wembley is a bigger, redder, more expensive version of all our other new stadia. Surely our national stadium should be more than that? Sticking an arch on top of it can't hide the fact that it is just a larger version of Hull's KC Stadium.

I am not asking for grounds to be built on mountaintops – West Brom's Hawthorns is widely known as the highest ground above sea level in England and I have never really understood how that is because it isn't on top of a mountain

– just for the men and women who design and locate them to show a bit of imagination and foresight and maybe, just maybe, put the fan first. Yes, it is great that at these grounds you have decent legroom, you don't have to queue twenty minutes for a wee (except at Wembley: eight hundred million quid and the bogs are still crap), and that no matter where you are sat you have a fantastic view and are not stuck behind a pillar. But we want more than that. We want passion and noise and colour and excitement.

The lack of passion and noise is blamed on the fans too. The game is too expensive nowadays so the fans are older and more middle class and less inclined to chant and sing. That's one theory. I, of course, have another one.

Away Fans

To travel to a game as an away fan is usually a more enjoyable experience than going to a home game. It is an adventure. It isn't an adventure in the Indiana Jones sense of the word. This is an adventure that involves minibuses, scarves hanging out the window, Ginsters, the odd can, plenty of songs, laughter, tears, more Ginsters, hopefully three points, an argument over who is going to drive home when you are all knackered, and then last orders. Of course it is a slightly different adventure if it is just you and your six-year-old going to an away game. That one tends to involve more sweets and less argument over who is going to drive home.

Because it is an adventure and it takes a bit of effort and planning to be an away fan, when you get to the opposition's ground you are feeling superior to all the home supporters who have just had to roll out of bed and they are in their seats. If I was a non-Manchester United fan I would put in the obvious joke here that this wouldn't of course be the case at Old Trafford where all the fans would have driven up from Surrey. Hilarious.

Once inside the ground and in your away fans section, the camaraderie begins. You are the hardcore fans who watch your side away as well as at home. You love your side more than the ones who just go to home games because you are spending more of your hard-earned cash on the team. You are the ones who know all the chants and all the words because you sing them more on away trips than you do at home. You are the loyal ones who love your club more than anybody else in the whole wide world, and you want to demonstrate this to the home fans in the ground.

The best way to demonstrate this is to chant and sing at the home end. Where is it, though? To see it, you have to crane your necks or turn ninety degrees, but then you can see them but you can't see the pitch. Why? Because more and more, the away fans are not given an 'end'. They are instead given 'a side bit' or 'a corner' or 'a space that is the crappest part of the ground but it will have to do because we want our home fans to have all the best bits of the ground'.

At Old Trafford, the away fans are housed right in the corner on the middle tier. From my seat it is actually quite difficult to see them. White Hart Lane is another ground where the fans are tucked away in the corner. Villa Park has now gone down the route of Goodison Park where the away fans are now at the side of the pitch rather than at one end. Both these grounds are what I would term 'proper' football grounds, of the kind you would find in Germany, and both used to be great grounds for the away fan because you would have an 'end', although I think you would have to go back to the days of standing to get an 'end' at Goodison.

Now, though, the away fans at both these grounds are tucked away elsewhere, treated as a nuisance, in much the same way you stick an elderly relative in the corner of a room after Christmas dinner. You are aware that they are there but you really don't want to engage with them, particularly if they have been at the sprouts. Except we should want to engage with the away fans.

Immediately the home fans have one end and the away fans the other, the atmosphere is ratcheted up several decibels. The ninety minutes of a game turns into a see-saw of noise as the chants go back and forth because fans know where to aim their songs. When you are an away fan tucked into a corner, who do you actually sing your semi-abusive ditties at? Do you aim them at the home fans nearest to you? Do you aim them at the home fans at the nearest end of the ground to you? Or do you aim them at the 'home end'? Different people have different aims. It's hard enough trying to coordinate a song without having to coordinate the direction you are going to sing it in. So in the end you are all singing it in different directions, which just dilutes the effect.

When I went to Chelsea a few years back, there was very little chanting from the United fans that summer evening. This was partly for the reasons I have explained above, but also because it was very difficult to see what was happening on the pitch. In their brilliance, the Stamford Bridge hierarchy had decided at that time to house the away support behind the benches. So not only did you have to watch the game through the clear Perspex of the dugout, you also had to bob and weave as various substitutes, managers, coaching staff, kit managers, physios and a few hangers-on – the sort you see every week on the bench but never know what they actually do – got up and down. I basically paid £45 to watch the back of José Mourinho's head, and I don't care how special he is, he isn't worth that. It was as if someone at Chelsea had thought, 'We've got seats with a shit view, what should we do with them? I know! We'll put the away fans there.'

There are still football clubs that keep the fans at one end of the ground – Liverpool, West Ham, Sunderland and Birmingham are just a few that come to mind. Although when I say one end, I don't mean the whole of one end, just part of it. Fans only seem to get the whole of one end in FA Cup games, where the away club has to receive a higher allocation of tickets. The Cup games I have been to over the past few years have tended to have a better atmosphere than league games. Portsmouth in the Cup at Old Trafford is bouncing compared to Portsmouth in the league because there are thousands more of them and they take over two tiers at the K Stand end of the ground. The noise increases, the banter increases, and the home fans in the Stretford end have to raise their game because of the massed blue ranks opposite them.

Back to the league games, though, and the clubs that allocate only part of one end to the away support. They will always give the home fans part of that end as well, and if possible they will try to make sure that the home fans have the part of the stand that is behind the goal. If they can't do that then they will try to make sure that the tarpaulin (usually green) used to separate the fans is behind the goal instead. They will do everything in their power to make sure that the away fans are not directly behind the net. Why? Because it is a lot more difficult to give the home keeper some stick when you aren't behind a goal.

I am not advocating hurling abuse down on a man wearing some garish kit and oversized gloves, but if the home fans are going to make my goalkeeper feel uncomfortable when he has to stand in front of them for forty-five minutes then I would like the opportunity to do the same to theirs. He will hear the chants of 'England's number 10' or 'City reject' a lot more easily if the away fans are right behind him rather than forty yards to his right. It also makes fetching the ball for a goal kick a lot easier because he doesn't have to look into the whites of the eyes of the away fans (or the reds of the eyes if it has been a long away trip and they have had a few ales).

It also prevents that hilarious joke away fans enjoy when the ball has been smashed into their midst by their own striker who couldn't hit a barn door. The home keeper then stands in front of this massed horde of the enemy, asking for the ball back so that he can take the goal kick. The joker in the pack keeps hold of the ball so that the keeper has to ask a ball boy or the referee for another ball. One is found for him, and he places it on the corner of the six-yard box and steps back ready to hoof. At this point the joker throws the original ball back on to the pitch, causing huge hilarity in the ranks of the away fans and no reaction from the keeper, who has found the whole thing tiresome.

So far, we have had away fans in a corner, away fans at the side, away fans with crap views behind the dugouts, and away fans given part of an end but not the whole of one end. However, there is one club in this country, one club in all of England, Scotland and Wales, that can surpass all others with the location it has chosen for the away support at their ground. There is no danger of not being able to see past a dugout or keep the ball from the goalkeeper when you are three miles up in the sky at St James's Park, Newcastle.

An away trip to Newcastle would be one of the best in the country if you didn't actually have to watch your team. The stadium is imposing and bright, the city itself a joy to be in, the nightlife like nothing I have experienced in any other UK city. You will not lack for choice when it comes to bars, pubs and clubs, and contrary to what a certain Newcastle board member once said about the female population of the city, they are not dogs. They are quite the opposite: they have a tendency to show a fair amount of flesh and all seem to have amazing tans considering they live in the north-east of England, not the Costa del Sol. But all of that cannot hide the fact that the football club has the worst away section in the country.

The website Football Ground Guide gives helpful hints and tips for away fans about the grounds they are visiting. It offers this advice if you are planning on seeing your team at Newcastle: 'if you are scared of heights or have poor eyesight then this may not be for you'. To reach the away section at St James's Park you have to go up fourteen flights of stairs. Fourteen! It's a bigger climb than the one to get to

Kaiserslautern's stadium. The website goes on to say, 'On the plus side, you do get a wonderful view of the whole stadium, plus the Newcastle skyline and countryside in the distance.' That's all right then. I can't actually see my team on that green thing way down below but I can get a lovely view of the smog rising over Middlesbrough.

Maybe Newcastle could change things round for a couple of seasons and put the away fans somewhere else. They could then use that section for all the fat topless lads we see every single time Newcastle are on the telly. Imagine how quickly those bellies and moobs would disappear if they were climbing up fourteen flights of stairs every other week.

Somebody within football did give me another reason why Newcastle situate the away support where they do: they are less likely to influence the referee from up in the gods. Imagine the visiting striker powering into the penalty area whereupon he gets clattered by a Newcastle defender. The away support are up as one, clamouring for a penalty, but the official has to have the hearing of a bat to pick up their noise. Also, I am no physicist, but by the time the sound waves have travelled the three miles from stand to pitch, the game has moved on by about two minutes, and the referee is left wondering why the away fans are cheering the award of a throw-in so loudly.

The real plus side to being an away fan at St James's is that they do a great chicken balti pie, and they are becoming harder and harder to get hold of.

Products on Sale

Pies, crisps, beer, chocolate, burgers, hot dogs, sausage rolls, Bovril, coffee and sweets. The football club menu would cause Jamie Oliver to have a heart attack. It could cause anyone to have a heart attack just looking at it, but Jamie would be furious at its lack of culinary goodness and its promotion of unhealthy eating. In defence of football, these things are something you would indulge in on a weekly basis at the match, not what you would eat on a daily basis, like Jamie assumes the people of Rotherham do.

However, to the chagrin of football supporters but probably to the delight of our favourite cockney wunderkind chef, the menus at our clubs are changing and the choice is dwindling. This is not down to the healthy do-gooders in today's society (I know a burger is bad for me but I like one occasionally, so if you could just stick that roasted pepper where the sun don't shine) but because of the rise of the official club partner.

I don't know about you, but whenever I am on Merseyside I always feel like I could kill for a pint of Chang beer. That thirst for a premium Thai beer increases if I go to Goodison Park, so thank the Lord that that is the beer on offer within the ground because of Everton's shirt sponsorship. A similar thing occurs to me at Old Trafford. I never feel like a Boddingtons when I arrive at United, despite it being the Cream of Manchester and me wanting to conform to a Manc stereotype. Instead I always get a thirst for an American beer I have never particularly liked the taste of. I immediately want to walk up to the counter, bellow 'whaaaaaaaaaasup' at the surly youth behind said counter and order a Bud.

Budweiser, if you didn't know, has, according to a press release, 'the exclusive lager pouring rights at Old Trafford so adult supporters can enjoy the crisp, clean and refreshing taste of the King of Beers at every game'. What a relief it is to know that my club offers up exclusive lager pouring rights. We could really be in the shit if they didn't do that. We might even have a choice of beers to enjoy before the game if they didn't do that. Do they offer up exclusive coffee bean grinding rights? Get in there quick, Kenco. As I write, are Fruit Gums and Fruit Pastilles involved in a heated bidding war to win the exclusive chewy fruity sweet franchise for the next three years?

As well as offering up all the products associated with the 'official partners' of your club, there is also a willingness to improve the fare on offer to us, the fans. Roy Keane's 'prawn sandwich' comment will never be forgotten as a way of referring to the corporate hospitality set, but in a lot of grounds now you don't get something as common as a prawn sandwich in the normal sections of the ground, let alone in the posh bits. Sandwiches are so 1990s. Now it is all about paninis, ciabattas, focaccias, bagels and wraps. They aren't filled with cheese and tomato or cheese and pickle, but goats' cheese and sun-dried tomatoes, or old farmhouse cheddar with onion relish. A seafood wrap is the new prawn sandwich. A seafood wrap can also cost a few quid more than a prawn sandwich. Fancy words, fancy descriptions, fancy products, fancy prices. A pie and a pint in a twenty-first-century football ground? Not a chance. If you want to keep it real, you have to visit a burger van on the way to the ground. And with that comes a real risk of the runs.

I have even heard vicious rumours – and these are quite unbelievable; in fact I am probably running the risk of being sued by even repeating these vile accusations, but I feel it is my duty to report them – I have heard that in some grounds they are serving . . . pasta salads. Not in corporate hospitality, but in the over-the-counter outlets. Pasta salads? A football ground is not the equivalent of a Marks and Spencer on a train station forecourt and should never be treated as such. Instead of plastic bottles of ketchup and mustard on a table at the side, I am assuming there will be balsamic vinegar and extra virgin olive oil, the extra virgin olive oil being a compromise to some good old-fashioned working-class innuendo. And in all of this, the pasta salad will cost more than the bag of chips it replaced on the menu and is therefore a greater 'revenue earner', as I believe the businessmen like to say. I haven't even dared to investigate whether the standard cup of coffee is being replaced at every ground by the latest frothy moccafroppacappa-mocchichachichocaccino.

Maximizing revenues is the mantra of every stadium in twenty-first-century football, and posh food and official partners are only a couple of ways of doing that. If chips, pies and ale are going by the wayside then so is another traditional staple of the old grounds, and they are being replaced by something that can seriously damage your health. Well, give you a headache at least.

Moving Advertising Boards

'The market is worldwide,' the executive chairman of Manchester City Gary Cook recently stated. 'There's something not right about sitting in a bar in Bangkok, Beijing or Tokyo and seeing "Fred Smith's Plumbing. Call 0161 . . ." Are we maximizing the central entity of the Premier League?'

I find it difficult to answer the question 'Are we maximizing the central entity of the Premier League?' because I don't actually understand it. I am assuming it means 'Are we bringing in shedloads of money to our club and exploiting fans all over the world?' 'Exploiting' is probably a little bit harsh, so maybe I should dip into marketing speak and say something like 'maximizing the cash potential of fans all over the world'. Cook would probably prefer that phrase. He used to be a big boss at Nike. Can you tell?

If I find the second part of his quote difficult to understand, then I find the first part deeply saddening. When you go to a ground, sit in your seat and look round the place, is your first thought 'I wonder how this looks on telly in

China'? If it isn't then you won't make it into the higher echelons of a Premier League club boardroom.

I would suggest to Cook that there is something not right about sitting in a stadium just a couple of miles outside Manchester city centre and seeing adverts aimed at a Far East market, sometimes in their language. It must make Liam and Noel weep into their parkas.

A football club has always been at the heart of the community, whichever club it is. It gives the people who support it a sense of belonging and pride. Clubs take great care to build their relationships with the communities around them, often offering education programmes and other courses to help the less fortunate in society. Does it not therefore have a duty to help local businesses? Clubs are not charity cases of course, local businesses should not get free advertising, but if Fred Smith pays for his pitch at Eastlands, should his plumbing business not be supported by the club? As soon as you drop down the leagues, local firms sponsor players, shirts, balls and matchday hospitality. Everybody benefits, and it maintains a vital link between the club and the business community. Premier League clubs are in effect flicking the Vs to hard-working local men and women and chasing the dollar, or rather the yen and the renminbi.

That is probably going to be the deepest, most serious paragraph of the whole book because the effect on the local community doesn't annoy me nearly as much as the method by which the global brands that will appeal to the Far East are being marketed in the big grounds – moving advertising boards.

Gone are the old wooden boards with Fred the Plumber's number on them. The perimeter of the pitch is now a blur of colour and signs and language and movement. Players of yesteryear often wish they were playing in the modern game, money being the prime reason for that desire. I can guarantee, though, that Bryan Robson would buck that trend. At least twice a season in the 1980s, Captain Marvel would career off the Old Trafford pitch and into an advertising board. This would normally result in a dislocated shoulder and six or seven weeks out. In this millennium, he would be careering off, dislocating his shoulder and electrocuting himself in the process as he went head first into a sign offering the latest official club ringtone.

This is what you are fed on these boards, the latest club ringtone, magazine, website and corporate hospitality packages mixed in with a couple of messages in Chinese or Thai, an advert for your club's community projects, and one from Sky saying how great they are. They are on a loop, and during a particularly boring game you can find yourself watching them rather than the action.

No matter who you support, we all have a player at our club who we know is a bit suspect in the concentration department. You always have to pray that the board isn't about to change message when the ball goes towards this player because he probably has one eye on the game and the other on the amazing hospitality package he could buy for his mates at the reasonable price of the equivalent of a small bungalow.

If it can confuse a player on the pitch then it also confuses me, but only when I am watching a match on television. When you watch a Champions League game, all the advertising is centrally controlled by UEFA so you get the standard messages from their official partners. However, when England play abroad, or there is a UEFA Cup (or Europa League or whatever it is now called) match, the rules are different and the advertising is up for grabs.

I am in my lounge watching Everton in UEFA Cup action with a beer in hand (not Chang). It is a tricky away tie in Romania against a decent side. I know this because I read a preview of the game in the paper that morning and also because Colin Murray and Pat Nevin are presenting the game from a studio in London and are not overlooking the ground. If Everton were at home then they would be at Goodison Park. Yet during the first half, in one fell swoop I am immediately confused and swathed in self-doubt as to who is at home and who is the away team. All because the electronic boards are showing an advert for Five's late film. Why are they advertising *Confessions of a Window Cleaner* at 10.55 on Five in a Romanian stadium? It is purely for us, i.e. the television audience, not fans of smutty seventies films. It has no regard for the spectators in the stadium. They will either be in a state of confusion or, if they love Robin Asquith, furious that they won't be able to see it.

The same thing happens when England are away and on ITV. You can see them plugging Corrie, the Nation's Street, just as Gareth Barry tries to control the ball on a very bumpy pitch in Azerbaijan. They love the witty banter between Rita and Norris on the streets of Baku.

Whether it is adverts here aimed at the Far East or the latest goings-on in a soap on a board in Eastern Europe, it is all aimed at the television audience. Except a lot of that audience complain about them. They are too distracting, and in the case of my mum, they give her a headache. They are here to stay though. They are too lucrative to be ditched, and on a moving board you can get so many more messages than on a static one. I just wish that Fred Smith's Plumbing appears on one of them one day. They need plumbers in Asia as well as here, you know.

THE
GAME

Tackling

It's not allowed, is it? Shall we move on to the next section?

It would be possible to leave it there with no further explanation necessary, but there is a word limit to reach so I will elaborate. As soon as a player falls over, in the Premier League in particular, the whistle goes and a free kick is given. It is easy to immediately point the finger at the referee. They don't understand the game because they have never played it – that's the common response of pundits. But the players themselves should accept the main responsibility for tackling turning into a dying art. If they weren't flinging themselves to the floor at the slightest touch – and we will come to diving later on – then the referee would find it easier to differentiate between a foul and a crunching tackle.

And there is nothing better than a crunching tackle. You can take your flicks and tricks, your nutmegs and stepovers, your volleys and scissor kicks, because there is nothing that gets the adrenalin running quite like a crunching tackle.

When anything happens on a football pitch, the crowd will make a relevant noise, no matter how big or small that crowd is. So even if you were outside the stadium, you could make an educated guess at what was happening inside just by the noises you were hearing. The loudest cheer is for a home goal; it is an explosion of ecstasy and joy. A hail of anger and abuse signals a bad decision by the referee, and a sharp intake of breath normally indicates the moment just before Paul Scholes launches himself into a 'tackle'. My favourite crowd noise, though, is that of thousands of people wincing. That means there has been a crunching tackle.

A crunching tackle is not an illegal tackle. It is not a 'leg-breaker'. It is a tackle that is full-blooded, where both players are determined to win that ball. Their eyes and thoughts are only on that ball and not on each other. They are becoming a rare sight in English football. It is not just Arsène Wenger who doesn't see them.

There are three sports that Ben likes to play in the garden or in the park with me: football, cricket and rugby (league, not union, because although he was born in the south I will make a Northerner of him yet). We will leave cricket out of it, though, because it really shouldn't involve physical contact between the players. When we play rugby, Ben will fly into tackles on me and I will fly into tackles on him. In each instance he is up after the tackle and ready to go again. When we play football, the slightest contact between the two of us and he is either screaming 'foul', 'free kick', or rolling over several times on the ground, holding his leg. Now, the odd tackle from me might verge on the side of hard (he has to learn, even at the age of seven), but his reaction is as informative as it is sad and pathetic. Yes, I do take these games with him very seriously.

When Ben watches rugby on television – either code – he sees massive men knocking the living daylights out of one another. In virtually every single case, they then get up. On the odd occasion they don't get up, they have been hit so hard that they don't roll around, they just lie there poleaxed. When he watches football, he sees players who feel the slightest contact hitting the ground then rolling, rolling, rolling. He therefore learns that if you are playing football, that is what you do, and if you are playing rugby, you just get on with it. And if you can knock Daddy out in a tackle in the process, even better.

'Learn' is a most appropriate word to use because tackling is not something you can just do. There is an art to tackling. It has to be learnt in the same way as swerving the ball, or a stepover, or a one-two. The game would be a poorer place without any of these skills. So why do so many players want to eradicate tackling through their actions?

It has to be down to a 'win at all costs' mentality. Ben throws himself to the floor because he assumes he will get a free kick. That, after all, is what he sees happening when he goes to games or watches football on TV. Players know now that if they are in a tussle for the ball and they hit the ground, 90 per cent of the time the decision will go their way. Referees are in a mindset that states a player on the ground equals a fall, which equals a free kick.

It is very easy to look at the past through rose-tinted glasses, and I am trying to make sure that I do not do that in this book. Well, not too much at least. I remember players diving in the eighties, and I grew up hearing tales of the players who dived in the sixties and seventies, but I honestly can't recall free kicks being given as soon as a player hit the turf, or footballers falling over every time they were tackled.

A couple of seasons ago I watched Phil Neville execute a stunning tackle on Cristiano Ronaldo. On a sun-drenched afternoon at a tempestuous Goodison Park, Neville slid in to try and win the ball. He went in with just the one foot and with no studs showing, but with a fair amount of force. He cleanly took the ball, putting it out for a throw-in, but his momentum took him into the Manchester United 7. You don't have to be Miss Marple, heck you don't even have to be Rosemary and Thyme, to work out what happened next. Ronaldo threw himself a good four or five feet in the air, pirouetting in the process, while at the same time grimacing and letting out an ear-splitting howl.

Neville was booked.

The decision infuriated me. Neville had done everything you are taught to do as a kid. He hadn't gone in two-footed, he hadn't shown his studs, but he had gone in with one hundred per cent commitment. Ronaldo hadn't. He had hung back, realizing that Neville was favourite. Just in case you are under eleven and tackling does somehow survive in the future, never ever hang back in a tackle. If you go in at one hundred per cent then you are less likely to be injured than someone who only goes in at seventy per cent or just dangles a leg into a tackle in the vain hope of winning the ball. Dangling your leg, I was always taught, is the easiest way to end up with a broken leg.

A former referee tried to explain the decision to me

afterwards, although he had a tough job because I was so incensed. He reasoned that Neville was booked because his momentum carried him into Ronaldo. His momentum? So, in order to avoid a booking, Neville would have had to calculate his stopping distance like a learner driver on a theory test before going into the tackle. Also, his momentum wouldn't have been a problem if Ronaldo hadn't hung back from the tackle and had gone into it in the same full-blooded manner.

The referee couldn't convince me; in fact his argument made me even more annoyed. If he had instead argued that the reason Neville received a yellow card might have been down to the shadow managers' reactions cast over the game, and in particular the giant shadows cast by the managers of the so-called Big Four, then it might have been more believable. Sir Alex Ferguson couldn't complain to the referee in that game about Ronaldo not receiving protection because Neville had been booked for his tackle on the Portuguese winger.

Referees must know deep down that if they don't take any action if anybody tackles any Arsenal player then they will incur the wrath of Arsène Wenger. Similarly, if players get stuck in to Steven Gerrard or Fernando Torres, Rafael Benitez will go a lovely shade of puce unless the cards are dished out. The players and the managers have created a fear culture among the referees. They would rather give the free kick or the yellow card than deal with the aftermath of letting things go, and who can blame them? A quick blow on the whistle, or nothing and then a gobful from Fergie, both up close and in the media? It really is no contest.

So, can we rescue tackling before it becomes obsolete? I am not so sure. As long as football continues to refer to itself as a multi-billion-pound business and not a sport then tackling will become as rare as Robin Van Persie staying fit for an entire season. Until the last five or six years, players always tackled, players often fell to the ground, players sometimes got injured. It is an accepted risk of the job. Or it *was* an accepted risk of the job. It was accepted when players weren't transferred for eight-figure sums, when qualifying for certain competitions didn't bring in £50 million to the club coffers.

I watched the Gillingham against Rochdale League Two play-off semi-final at the end of the 2008/09 season. It was refereed by Michael Oliver, who was only twenty-three at the time. Tackles flew in, the players got on with it, and Oliver let the game flow. Yes, it was a big game, and yes, the players needed protecting, but there wasn't the same massive financial pressure that there is in top-flight football. If Oliver had let two or three tackles go and then the Gillingham striker was crocked on the fourth, the repercussions would not have been as huge as letting two or three tackles go in a Real Madrid match and then Ronaldo getting crocked. I would imagine that an eighty-million-pound winger's insurance details are very different to a striker's in deepest Kent.

As tackling disappears, so too does one of the characters of the game. A character loved more by the fans than the skilful fancy dans or the thirty-a-year goal machine. The hardman is becoming redundant. The hardman isn't a thug. He doesn't feature on a DVD release that celebrates violence on the pitch and on the terraces but dresses itself up as entertainment and features several 'reformed' characters. The hardman isn't Vinnie Jones. The hardman is a footballer who can play but who also has steel and knows how to tackle. He can handle himself without resorting to violence.

I am talking about men like Steve McMahon, Bryan Robson, Peter Reid, Patrick Vieira, Roy Keane (Alf Inge Haaland might disagree with his inclusion), Paul Ince, Stuart Pearce and Graeme Souness, because if you look through the squads of Premier League sides now, that sort of player isn't there any more. Try and think of a top-flight hardman play-ing today. It's tough, isn't it? It's all about holding midfielders now. Everybody is looking for the player who can break up attacks by being in the right place at the right time, and then give it simply. They aren't looking for players who can thunder into tackles.

If the money and the rewards are overseeing the demise of the art of tackling and the best exponents of the art, then the win-at-all-costs mentality is encouraging the rise of the darkest art of the game and the players who practise it.

Diving

I am fortunate to be writing this section during a week in which Arsène Wenger has gone apoplectic. That in itself does not really narrow things down because most days when I've been writing Wenger has been angry about something or other. This week, however, he has been getting very, very angry about diving.

For the past twenty-five years, whenever a player dived you heard the shout from somewhere: 'Who does he think he is? The new Greg Louganis?' It didn't matter whether it was a professional game or a park game, as soon as a player dived, somebody would refer to the gold-medal-winning American diver from the 1984 and 1988 Olympics who is also well remembered for smacking his bonce on the springboard when he stuffed up one of his dives in Seoul. So, the week in which I am writing this is quite a momentous one, because I fear it is the moment when the Greg Louganis comment will stop being passed down from generation to generation. My son and all his friends won't be referring to an Olympic legend from two decades before they were born. No, when they dive – and they all do, even though they're only six and seven – they will be calling each other 'the new Eduardo'. In the space of this one week, he has dived to win a penalty in the Champions League against Celtic, become public enemy number one in every part of Scotland that doesn't support Rangers, and subsequently been banned by UEFA for two matches.

As Eduardo skipped clear of the Celtic defence, Artur Boruc came out to meet him. The Celtic goalkeeper realized that the Arsenal striker had pushed the ball too wide and too far so he pulled out of any challenge at the last moment. That left Eduardo with a choice: go down and try to win a penalty or let the ball run away from him for a goal kick. Given that this is a man who chose to play his international football for Croatia instead of Brazil and therefore chose to wear the red and white checked shirt over the famous yellow one, it won't surprise you to learn that he took the wrong option. He chose to dive.

But was it the wrong option? In the spirit of fair play and doing what is right, Eduardo did err. But if you are connected with Arsenal, his winning of the penalty took them one step closer to qualifying for the Champions League. That meant an autumn of top-class European football for the fans and the players and millions of pounds coming into the club for the board. Nobody was going to come out from the club and criticize the player when he helped them to the promised land, or the group stage as it is more commonly known.

The act of diving is abhorrent. The footballing authorities

call it 'simulation', which is too soft a word. It is cheating. Plain and simple. If you dive to win a free kick or a penalty or to try to get an opponent sent off then you are a cheat and you need to be treated as such. But how we react to such acts of treachery and deception is causing as much of a problem as the offence itself.

Cristiano Ronaldo, Robert Pires, Ruud Van Nistelrooy, Wayne Rooney, Steven Gerrard, Michael Owen and David Beckham. I have seen them all dive over the past ten years. Arsène Wenger never saw Robert Pires dive. Sir Alex Ferguson has never said he has seen Ronaldo or Van Nistelrooy go down too easily, or at least not in public. And the national press and media have never seen Owen, Gerrard, Rooney and Beckham do it on international duty. Or maybe they have, but they were diving for England so they didn't criticize them. That, unfortunately, is the crux of the matter. When players dive for your team it is all well and good; when they dive against you they are disgusting, disgraceful, dishonest cheats who should be banned, banned, banned. Eduardo's first game for Arsenal after the match with Celtic was against Manchester United at Old Trafford. He was a substitute. Every time he warmed up down the touchline he was greeted with shouts of 'cheat' from the home crowd. Strange. The same thing was never chanted at Ronaldo.

If just once after Ronaldo had gone over slightly easier than he should have done Fergie had come out and said he was out of order and he would be punished by the club, it would have been so refreshing. But he didn't. He would instead insist that 'the boy's sheer pace contributes to him falling over' or that 'he could see the tackle coming' and for that reason jumped out of the way. The 'could see the tackle coming' argument is a common excuse for diving that has been used by managers and pundits alike to excuse Beckham, Owen and Gerrard over the years.

Wenger also dipped into that cliché when discussing the Eduardo incident. As the striker had his leg horrifically broken eighteen months earlier, he is now more aware of when he is going to get clattered and therefore jumps out of the way accordingly, he argued. Even though you are fairly sure in your mind that that sounds like complete bollocks, you would have to be extremely harsh and hardnosed to argue back over a man who suffered such a stomach-churningly bad injury.

If you support the blue half of Manchester then you are probably nodding smugly at all these comments about Ronaldo and Van Nistelrooy, even Beckham. Well, stop right there. Let's not forget that one of your former players is the Godfather of Diving. He was also the King of Bog Roll after he founded a paper recycling business after quitting the game. But it was his ability to tumble here, there and everywhere that he is best known for. Step forward, and try not to deliberately trip yourself up as you do so, Francis Lee. Franny Lee is proof that this is the only section in the book which shows that the game hasn't changed in the thirty-six years of my life. There was diving in the seventies just as there is diving now.

Squat is the best way to describe Lee. Squat but immensely talented. His career took in Bolton, Manchester City and

Derby County, and he scored ten times in twenty-seven appearances for England. He was a penalty taker, and in 1971/72 he set a British record for the number of spot kicks he scored from in one season. Fifteen of his thirty-five goals came from penalties, which earned him the nickname Lee One Pen. Most of those penalties resulted from fouls committed on him, and a large proportion of the footballing community felt he may have dived to get some of them. Hence some parts of the media changed his nickname to Lee Won Pen.

I wasn't yet born in that season and I don't remember watching Lee play so it is a bit difficult to comment on how he acted. Looking at his physique, though, I am surprised he went over so easily because he resembles a Weeble, and we all know that 'Weebles wobble but they don't fall down'. However, if Norman Hunter's reaction to Lee winning a penalty in a game in 1975 between Derby and Leeds is anything to go by, diving angered people in the seventies as much as it does today. Blimey, there were some punches thrown in that game. Make sure you YouTube it.

If there is a difference between diving in the seventies and now, it is that it's more prevalent today and we see more of it. There are numerous cameras at every game, there are extra-super-slow slow-mo replays, and football from all over Europe is beamed into our living rooms and pubs so that we now see all those cheating foreigners diving every day of the year rather than every two years at a major international tournament. The old-school English mentality is that having more foreigners in our game leads to more diving because that 'is what they do' and also because our brave boys learn from them. Alternatively, and this is more likely, the rewards in the game are now so much greater. And when the rewards get greater, it is human nature to do whatever it takes to grab hold of them.

Put yourself in the position of a manager. If you don't win a specific game and fail to qualify for Europe then there is a high chance you will get the sack. In the game, your centre-forward dives to win a penalty. It is successfully converted, you hold on for a 1–0 win, you qualify for Europe and you keep your job. Are you honestly then going to come out and meet the press and condemn your striker for how he won the penalty when he kept you in the job? Course you aren't. It would be as hypocritical as a Miss World contestant saying she wants world peace and to save the rainforest when really she just wants to beat all the other jealous swimsuited cows alongside her.

We hope that our managers will be honest enough to take a stand against diving when we as fans don't. We will still cheer and back our own players who dive and boo the ones from the opposing side that do exactly the same thing because that is what we do. Players won't be honest, managers won't be honest and fans won't be honest, which only leaves the administrators. They have tried to tackle simulation. Eduardo was banned for two games, and in September 2007 Lithuania striker Saulius Mikoliunas was banned for two matches after video evidence showed he dived to earn a penalty against Scotland. So, UEFA have taken action against two players in two years. Do you think they are the only ones to have dived in that period? A two-game ban for diving does send out the right message, but only if it is consistently applied. UEFA, consistent as ever (more on them and FIFA later), changed their minds about Eduardo after Arsenal appealed. What message does that send out?

In the cases of Mikoliunas and Eduardo, the referee didn't see a dive because he awarded penalties. If a referee does see a dive then he will book a player. That is a massive inconsistency straight away. Get caught on the pitch, yellow card. Get caught by the TV cameras, two-game ban. Is a player who dives in a League Two game any less guilty than a player who dives in the Premier League or Champions League? As Bill Clinton might have said to Monica Lewinsky, how far down do you go? If you are going to tackle diving then you are going to have to include all the lower leagues to get the message across, and that is not just the lower leagues in this country, it is all the lower leagues in every UEFA member state from Albania to Scotland, Iceland to Turkey. Imagine all that paperwork.

I was always taught at school when writing an essay that you do your introduction, set out your arguments, then reach a conclusion. I think I have failed on this subject. I cannot reach a clear conclusion because diving is not black and white. It is a blur of conflicting arguments, thoughts and behaviour that is impossible to unravel. I would love to ban everybody who dives and eradicate it from the game. But a combination of money and human behaviour makes me fear that it would be impossible. Whoever first came up with 'honesty is the best policy' had obviously never worked in modern-day football. Or, for that matter, ever tried to write a chapter on diving.

Injuries

One of the greatest footballers of his generation hit the deck, and hit it hard. His hands rose to cover his face and, in obvious agony, the most famous yellow shirt in world football crumpled. It was 3 June 2002 in Ulsan, South Korea, and the man who had won the FIFA World Player of the Year and the European Footballer of the Year three years earlier had just ensured that he would no longer be best remembered for winning those two awards. He also scored in five consecutive games in that tournament as he helped Brazil win the World Cup, but if you mention 'Rivaldo' and 'World Cup' to any football fan, or maybe even just 'Rivaldo', they won't come back to you with 'World Cup winner', they will come back with 'World Cup cheat', or probably just laugh.

Standing by the flag, waiting to take a corner, the Brazilian playmaker, wearing the iconic number 10 shirt, had the ball whacked at him by the Turkish player Hakan Unsal. Rivaldo fell to the ground clutching his face. Except the ball never touched his face. It didn't even connect with the top half of his body. It barely bounced off his bottom half. It merely brushed his thigh. His disgraceful reaction – and it was nothing short of a disgrace – resulted in Hakan Unsal being sent off. Rivaldo was later fined ten thousand Swiss francs for his play-acting.

Play-acting and feigning injury is something FIFA have done their best to clamp down on over the past fifteen years. Back in the nineties, they introduced the rule that if a player was injured on the pitch and needed treatment then that had to take place off the field of play. The only exception was if the injured player was the victim of a tackle that had warranted a yellow card. In that case the player could be treated on the field, although they have since ditched that part. In theory it doesn't sound too bad, and you would like to think that a player would think twice about feigning an injury if he was going to be off the pitch and leaving his team a man short. That's in theory. In practice it is a bloody shambles. The rule somehow seems to have managed to penalize players who are genuinely injured and reward teams that commit fouls, which I am fairly sure was never FIFA's intention.

The shambles is a result of two things: a lack of knowledge of the laws of the game and a lack of common sense.

A foul is committed that results in a player rolling around on the ground. Because the referee doesn't think the tackle was too heavy, he isn't convinced the player grimacing at his feet is actually injured so he tells him to get up. The player refuses. The trainer is called on. He looks at the player and signals to his bench that he will be OK to continue. Meanwhile the ref is starting to get mardy and is telling both player and trainer to get off the pitch to continue treatment. They argue back but eventually are persuaded to move to the touchline, at which point they are joined by a member of their own coaching staff and the 4th official to check everything is done properly.

As soon as they are off the pitch, the injured player normally stands up, having had no treatment, and is ready to come back on. Player and trainer and coach all start signalling to get him back on while the 4th official tries to hold them back. The referee studiously ignores them all and concentrates on restarting the game. As soon as that happens, the player, coach and trainer work themselves into a state of apoplexy trying to get the player back on. The referee still won't signal to allow him to come back on, probably because he knows the rules and needs to give it a few seconds before waving him on, but I think more likely because he is a bit pissed off with how they have all behaved, so like a parent with a toddler he is going to make them all wait until they can join in again.

There are now so many gestures flying around the pitch that you could be at a semaphore convention, if such a thing exists. The crowd are restless, the team with the 'injured' player are restless, the officials are restless because they are trying to make sure everybody abides by the rules, and the whole thing has taken five minutes and been a complete and utter waste of time.

I have an idea. When a foul occurs, the trainer comes on to treat the injured player by throwing some water over the hurt area of the body, sprays a bit of cold spray on it, then the player gets up, the free kick is taken and the game continues. The whole thing would last no more than ninety seconds.

Oh yeah, that's how it used to be done.

FIFA's intentions with this rule were honourable. It was designed to stop the Rivaldos of this world (although Rivaldo was off the pitch already when his catastrophic injury took place). Unfortunately, as I said, the rule can be incredibly unfair on players who are genuinely injured and can reward the team that committed the foul in the first place.

A player gets clattered in the centre circle. He is 6'4" and his side's best chance of a goal from set-pieces. The tackle isn't great and results in a free kick. The player gets injured as a result and after all the shenanigans has to leave the field for the magic spray. His team have a free kick, but their best chance of scoring from the ball they are about to launch into the box is off the field through no fault of his own. Not only have they lost him, they are reduced to ten men for the set play whereas the team that committed the foul are still at their full complement.

In an ideal world, you would rely on the goodwill and honesty of players only to go down injured when they are actually hurt. That's asking a lot, though, because as we have seen with diving, goodwill and honesty tend to be in short supply in the modern game, and actually, when we do rely on a bit of goodwill and honesty then we descend further into chaos.

There are few more heroic gestures in football than

kicking the ball into touch to allow a member of the opposite side to receive treatment. You are sacrificing possession and all that could come of it to allow a stricken opponent to get better. What could be simpler? What could indicate fair play better? What greater sign of morality and doing the right thing is there? What could football turn into a greater farce than this? 'Nothing' is the answer to all the preceding questions.

In December 2000, Paolo Di Canio produced an astounding act of sportsmanship at Goodison Park. The Everton goalkeeper Paul Gerrard was lying in a heap outside the penalty area. He had twisted his knee while attempting a clearance and was obviously in pain. As the cross came in to Di Canio, and with the goal at his mercy, the West Ham striker caught the ball. He wasn't going to score with a stricken keeper on the floor. His decision won him the FIFA Fair Play Award in 2001.

It is an unwritten rule in football that as soon as a player is down the ball must go straight out so he can receive treatment. It is something that has crept up on us over the years and is now accepted as some kind of official edict. But it isn't in any rule book. The referee must stop a game if there is a head injury because that obviously requires immediate treatment. Equally, in those horrific tackles where somebody's leg is pointing in two directions – think Arsenal's Eduardo or Coventry City's David Busst – then the players will stop the match immediately, normally because a couple of players in the vicinity of the injury are close to passing out at the sight of it. My sister was in the stands at Old Trafford when Busst suffered his injury, and despite being a fair distance away from the pitch she was nearly sick. Peter Schmeichel was so close to the unfortunate defender's horrible leg break that he went pale. His nose included. That's how bad it was.

So, prone goalkeepers, head injuries and badly broken legs are all clear-cut situations where there is no argument about stopping play. The waters get muddier when the 'injuries' are less obvious.

Eight and a half years on from Di Canio becoming the shining knight of fair play (an astonishing achievement given that he once pushed over a referee in a comical way and has made no secret of his far right sympathies in a definitely not comical way), Chelsea were playing Manchester United in the Charity – sorry, Community Shield (there is a big difference, although I know not what). Midway through the second half, Patrice Evra was poleaxed by Michael Ballack. With their left-back lying on the turf inside the Chelsea half, Manchester United played on. Their move eventually broke down and Chelsea broke forward. Some United players started gesturing for the ball to be kicked into touch so Evra could receive treatment. Moments later there was a break in play for the United physio to get on, because the ball had crossed over a white line. The goal line. Courtesy of Frank Lampard's boot and Ben Foster's limp wrist, it was in the back of the net. Chelsea celebrated, United fumed, Fergie went purple. Why United felt a sense of injustice I am not quite sure. *They* chose to play on with one of their own men on the floor so they couldn't then expect Chelsea to kick the ball out when they won it back.

Going down injured could now be considered as much a part of the tactical side of the game as defending set-pieces or attacking free kicks. If that sounds far-fetched then I challenge you to look me in the eye and tell me that your side, whether it is one you support or one you play for, has never done the following.

In the opposition half, there is a tackle. As a result of the clash the ball breaks to the opposition and your player is on the pitch. If he gets up and thinks about chasing back, he will be working from the opposition player having a fifteen-yard head start. The opposition are swarming forward, they are outnumbering your team. For that reason your player doesn't decide to get up and start the long chase back, he decides to stay on the floor and clutch his ankle, knee, shin, hip, wrist, arm, shoulder, head (delete as appropriate). Your team start screaming at the opposition, saying they have a man down and gesturing for them to kick the ball out. Your opponents are now confused. What should they do? They have an advantage but at the same time they are thinking of the unwritten rule. If this is being played in front of a crowd, there are howls of derision, boos and whistles the longer they keep hold of the ball. Eventually the pressure tells on one of them and he knocks the ball out. Cue whistles and boos from their fans at that decision and the physio running on to treat the 'injured' player.

Their attack has broken down and their chance has gone, but to reciprocate their fair play, they know they will get the ball back from your side. It is the gentlemanly thing to do. But do they get the ball back in the same position they kicked it out? Do they heck as like. Your team take the throw-in. The ball is thrown to a member of your team who more often than not, in the style of Jonny Wilkinson, knocks it forty yards back into the opposition half and out of touch. It has gone so beautifully towards the corner that you might as well resume with a lineout. The opposition have to resume trapped in their own half with a throw-in. At the same time, your 'injured' player jogs back on to the pitch, or, if he really wants to rub it in, sprints on. Not a scratch or a bruise on him.

Just like diving, it is a blatant form of cheating, and just like diving it is seeping into junior football. I don't know if you have ever watched under-sevens games – and it is not something I would recommend unless you are a parent because, to put it bluntly, it is shit. As a dad, I shouldn't say this. I should praise my boy and his team-mates for their effort and their skill. It really can be mind-numbing, though, as you watch a whole group of little people all chase after the same ball. At this point Ben would like to state that this description applies equally when he watches his dad's team play. Except they aren't little people and they are all fat. But they all chase the ball in the same way and it is equally mind-numbing. He doesn't say it is shit, though, because he hasn't learnt that word yet, but the day is not far off when he will start using it.

The one difference between the under-sevens and my team, however, is the number of times Ben's side will fall over or go down in a tackle and be hurt. They aren't putting it on, though. They really do believe that they have broken their legs when they have in fact just grazed their shins. It is understandable, because they are only little and children don't have the highest pain threshold. However, it does mean that the bloody ball is constantly being kicked into touch so that they can receive treatment. A junior game of football that should take forty minutes can last three hours because of all the injuries and confusion over who should give the ball back to whom.

Sometimes the matches can last even longer if they are high-scoring because every goal requires a celebration. And seven-year-olds are no different to the professionals. They love a good goal celebration.

Goal Celebrations

Aylesbury United Football Club and the Brazil World Cup-winning side of 1994 don't often get lumped together, but in my mind they are inseparable. They are both responsible for kicking off the craze of 'wacky' goal celebrations. Dealing with it chronologically, we will begin with Brazil.

The 1994 World Cup isn't a vivid one for me. None of the home countries had qualified and there was a fear that the tournament would be Americanized as it was being held in the USA. The Republic of Ireland were providing the most interest: they beat Italy in one match, and John Aldridge swore live on television during an altercation with a jobsworth over a substitution. That's how exciting it was. Throw in an astonishing elbow by the Brazilian Leonardo that fractured the skull of the American Tab Ramos and that's the limit of my memories going into the quarter-finals. Brazil's quarter-final against the Netherlands, however, provided my stand-out memory of the whole tournament.

There were some decent goals as Brazil won 3–2 with both sides bizarrely wearing their away strips, the Dutch in white, the Brazilians in dark blue. None of that is particularly memorable, though, unlike one of the goal celebrations. The little Brazilian striker Bebeto scored the second of his side's goals, a goal that put them 2–0 up. After rounding the goal-keeper and slotting the ball into the empty net he set off towards the corner flag in celebration. He put both his arms together, held them out in front of him and started rocking them. He was miming cradling a baby, because just a few days earlier his wife had given birth to his third child. As he stood there rocking away, he was joined by two team-mates, Romario and Mazinho, who started doing the same thing. The three of them were just stood there rocking away in perfect timing as a tribute to the arrival of a precious new-born into this world. It felt spontaneous, it was cute, it tugged at the heartstrings, and it started millions of bio-logical clocks ticking all over the planet.

If I was being a real curmudgeon, and also pernickety, I would have to say that one of my problems with it is that you don't actually cradle a baby like that. You tend to hold them into your body when you rock them, not out front on outstretched arms, and Bebeto should really have known this. Do not forget, this was his third child. He was an experienced parent, not fresh out of an NCT class. Still, as Bebeto celebrated it was fresh and new, and it demonstrated a father's love for his newborn. Romario and Mazinho's contribution was improvised, showing a desire to share in the joy of both their team-mate's goal and his fatherhood. The technicalities of rocking a baby aside, this goal celebration has now become one of the most copied and choreographed in world football. And it is now one of the most bloody annoying goal celebrations ever.

Fifteen years on, when I see it done, it provokes more questions than answers. Given that some footballers have a lot of love for a lot of ladies, and given that there are certain ladies who have had love for a lot of footballers, when I see this celebration now, my first thought is 'Who's the daddy?' It might be what some of the players are thinking. 'Christ, I'd better join in this celebration because I think I shagged her around nine months ago so it could be mine.' One best-selling red top reported recently that a Premier League striker had got three different women pregnant all in a short space of time. He is in serious danger of repetitive strain injury in nine months' time if he starts scoring a lot of goals.

Dubious morality aside, it is the fact that it is choreographed that winds me up more than anything else. How much of a training session was spent working out which corner the celebration would start in, who would join in and, most importantly, which direction the arms should rock in first? You need to be coordinated with this one. You don't want some rocking to the left at the beginning as others throw the arms to the right. It would be a shambles. To get it right, it has to be practised. Time has to be spent coordinating that routine. Time, I am fairly sure, that should be spent working out how to defend corners or improve your direct free kicks.

This is where Aylesbury United Football Club come in. A non-league side that devised the most coordinated, famous goal celebration of the past twenty years.

The season that immediately followed USA 94 saw

Aylesbury progress to the third round of the FA Cup – a creditable achievement considering they were playing at a level one below the Conference at the time. A Cup run guaranteed television exposure either on the BBC or Sky, with all the goals from all the games from the first round onwards being shown. Newport and Kingstonian were beaten in the first two rounds before a third-round clash against QPR at Loftus Road, where Aylesbury were beaten 4–0. The report on that third-round game on *Match of the Day* included a line from Ray Stubbs who said that the home fans were willing Aylesbury to score to see what celebration they had planned. Their goal celebrations had become more famous than anything else about them.

And what a celebration it was. In one of their earlier rounds, after scoring the whole team congregated together, got on their knees and waddled round the pitch led by the scorer. They were meant to look like ducks. Ducks who wore lovely green and white hoops and didn't have beaks, but ducks all the same. The reason? The club's nickname is The Ducks. Bugger their FA Cup run, Aylesbury United Football Club had raised the bar in terms of goal celebrations. Running away with one arm in the air while waiting to get the congratulations of your team-mates (yes, Alan Shearer, I'm talking about you) would no longer suffice. The Ducks had taken the Brazilian baby-cradling routine and run with it, or rather waddled with it. I imagine professional teams wandered into their training grounds on a Monday morning in January 1995 and had a serious debrief on how to celebrate a goal. They couldn't have these non-league upstarts leading the way. They weren't professionals. They had to hold down a proper job as well as their football yet they still came up with something as blinding as a waddling ducks routine. The gloves were off. It was time for the professionals to show the world what they were made of.

So since Aylesbury, and because of Aylesbury, we have had to put up with some of the most cringeworthy, embarrassing and downright dreadful 'team' goal celebrations. We have had players try to perform a dance routine (a favourite of Emmanuel Adebayor), which is not something that should be done unless everybody involved has rhythm and co-ordination (centre-halves should not try to get in on this one). We have had the dentist's chair from Euro 96, where Gazza was squirted with a water bottle by celebrating team-mates. There was a Nigerian routine which involved the goalscorer slapping each player in succession around the chops and them falling down like a set of dominoes, and of course there is the boot-shining one. This is where the scorer gets a team-mate to kneel down, he puts his boot on his thigh, and then another colleague comes along to shine the boot that scored the goal. It doesn't work as well if the goal has been scored with a header. I am sure you can think of many others, and all of them need rehearsal time. As your team perform the boot-shining routine, you do start wondering just how vigorous and tactically astute their last training session was.

While I sit and worry about this (quite a lot as you can see, and probably more than is healthy), FIFA and UEFA worry about the much more heinous crime of seeing a player's chest. The removal of the shirt is a yellow-card offence according to them. Seeing a well-toned six-pack and some decent pecs is not what the viewing public want to see apparently. I know plenty of people who disagree. The directive was brought in to try to stop messages being printed on vests underneath the shirts. The authorities took a dim view of these because they felt footballers could bring the game into disrepute, depending on what was written. Most of the time these messages carried the number of goals the player had scored for his team, or they were thanking the parents, the missus, the kids or God. God himself – well, the Liverpool version – once showed his support for the dockers on a vest when he scored a goal and that got him into all sorts of trouble. Mind you, I would rather see Robbie Fowler supporting the dockers than just taking his shirt off to reveal nothing underneath. And anyhow, Fowler was to get into more trouble for another celebration, which we will come to shortly.

Trying to take your shirt off in celebration can prove problematic, as we saw earlier with Diego Forlan, so some players resort to just pulling it over their faces. Fabrizio Ravanelli pioneered this celebration, I think to make sure he could never see Emerson's wet-look perm heading towards him for a cuddle.

But the shirt over the face is not the celebration for most footballers because it means people can't see them properly. To put it more accurately, photographers can't see them properly. There is no more perfect way to ensure all eyes are on you than to score a goal. David Beckham is the best exponent of the art of knowing exactly where the photo-grapher is and how he can get the best shot of just him without his team-mates sharing in his glory. If he headed to the corner and stood there with his arms outstretched then the snapper should just have to time to get a shot of him before he was jumped on. When Eric Cantona scored, everybody else knew not to go anywhere near him for the first ten seconds afterwards so that he could milk the crowd's applause on his own. If you don't believe me, think of his iconic, solitary pose after he scored a magnificent chip against Sunderland. 'Look at me, look at my talent, look at my collar,' he was saying. 'I am a class apart.' Andrew Flintoff now strikes a similar pose, without the collar, after taking crucial wickets for England.

Standing still and milking the applause is not for every-body, and individuals are constantly striving to come up with new and innovative celebrations. At the start of the 1994/95 season (what was it about that time and goal celebrations?), Jürgen Klinsmann endeared himself to the English public, which for a diving German was no mean feat. The best way to get the English to like you? Take the piss out of yourself. That is exactly what he did. He was known for diving, so when he headed his first goal for Spurs on his debut at Sheffield Wednesday he ran towards the touchline and dived across the wet turf. A love affair with the Spurs fans and England had begun.

A love affair with Peter Crouch began in a similar way. In the build-up to the 2006 World Cup, Crouch unveiled his robot dance after scoring in the sun at Old Trafford for

England. The media went crazy for it. Some papers included step-by-step guides to emulate it, and Crouch was asked to repeat it at every given opportunity. Dance like a nob and the English public adore you. Roger Milla had more rhythm when he danced round the corner flags at the World Cup in 1990; Lee Sharpe had more rhythm as he perfected the Sharpey Shuffle in the early nineties; yours truly had no rhythm as he tried to copy the Sharpey Shuffle in Preston after scoring a penalty against the University of Central Lancashire. I pulled my groin and had to be substituted.

Players now box corner flags (Tim Cahill). They try to make letters with their hands (Andy Johnson and Titus Bramble) like some kind of *Sesame Street* presenter. (The sign they were making was the letter A, to show their support for a project that helps young people. Admirable, but bloody difficult to make out when you are thirty rows back in the top tier.) There are players who kiss (Alan Smith and Gary Kelly), there are players who have imitated a dog having a pee (Nigeria's Finidi George and Paolo Di Canio), there are players who flip and somersault (Nani and Lua Lua), there's a player who just does a crappy somersault (Robbie Keane), and there are hundreds who kiss or slap the badge of the shirt they are wearing usually just before they ask for a transfer to a club that matches their ambitions.

The best one there has ever been, however, comes courtesy of Robbie Fowler. During a Merseyside derby, Fowler had been getting an almighty amount of stick off the Everton fans. There were plenty of chants about him being involved in or doing cocaine. So when he scored a penalty in front of them at the Anfield Road End, he got down on all fours and pretended to snort the goal line. It wasn't condoning drug use, he wasn't suggesting he did coke, it was just a response to what was being chanted at him. It was a spur-of-the-moment thing, and it was funny. Although not nearly as funny as Gérard Houllier suggesting afterwards that he wasn't pretending to snort the line but instead pretending to eat the grass. The authorities didn't get the joke. They saw it as offensive or illegal or both probably, and fined him £32,000. It was the price per gram of whitewash he had snorted.

I would rather they concentrated on the two goal celebrations that are massively offensive, and could cause riots when they are performed: the finger over the lips and the cupping of the ears. Both of them send the same message out to opposition fans: 'Shut up. I have scored.' Do what you like to us fans, but don't ever, ever tell us to be quiet. It winds us up more than anything else. Wayne Rooney once scored for Manchester United at Anfield and celebrated in front of the Kop by cupping his ears. Among the abuse hurled back at him was a mobile. It wasn't the smartest move by either Rooney or the phone chucker. Rooney because he was inciting the crowd, and the phone chucker because it would be quite easy to trace him through his phone. Celebrate with your own fans, celebrate with your own team-mates even if it is a shittily choreographed dance, or celebrate on your own to give a photographer a great shot, just don't wind up the oppo fans.

Oh yeah, and while we are on the subject of goals and celebrations, I don't need to hear the chorus of 'Chelsea

Dagger' by The Fratellis to know that the ball has hit the back of the net and that I should be up and out of my seat celebrating. Celebrating a goal should be an instinctive reaction, it shouldn't have to be taught, encouraged or choreographed.

Trophy Presentations

The 1981 FA Cup Final was the first Cup Final I can remember watching. It was between Spurs and Manchester City and afterwards I thought that all Cup Finals were going to be like that. I assumed that they would have great goals, there would be a replay if the first match had been drawn, the winning captain would always go up the famous Wembley steps to lift the trophy, and that it would never be won by Manchester City. Only one of those has remained a constant over the past twenty-seven years, and I would like to thank Manchester City for that.

It would have been impossible for every Final since then to have had great goals. I can also understand that replays have had to be sacrificed in such a packed footballing calendar. The last Final to go to a second game was in 1993, when Arsenal defeated Sheffield Wednesday thanks to a last-minute extra-time goal from Andy Linighan. What I have really missed is the disappearance of players going up the stairs to pick up the trophy.

Picking up the trophy used to be an event in itself. There

were thirty-nine steps up to the royal box at Wembley, as John Motson told us every single year, and they were right next to the fans. This meant that supporters could get so close to the players they could decorate them on their way up. The majority of players, when they reached the minor royal they had to shake hands with, looked like a cross between an athlete and *Coronation Street*'s Percy Sugden. There they were, for one of the crowning moments of their career, lifting the FA Cup in a multicoloured flat cap and scarf combo.

Different captains behaved in different ways before picking up trophies. In 1966, Bobby Moore respectfully wiped his hands on his kit and the velvet drape in the royal box so that they were free of dirt and grass before he shook hands with the Queen and received the Jules Rimet trophy. There have been other skippers who, forgetting where they are, have turned to their fans, lifted the FA Cup and screamed 'GET FUCKING IN!' There have been others who have lifted the Cup only to see the lid drop off and hit the team-mate stood behind them.

Despite the perils of being hit by parts of a trophy, second in line was always quite a prestigious place to be when picking up the FA Cup. Whoever was second normally got to carry the base of the trophy down to the on-pitch celebrations. The Cup itself would always be passed along the line so that everybody got to lift it in front of their fans, before the last person in the line brought it down the steps. The last person would either be the manager or the team's joker. The 'joker' would normally have collected so much memorabilia from the fans on his way up that by the time he lifted the Cup he looked like an advert for the club shop, wearing a comedy hat, four scarves, waving a couple of flags and pointing at his mum with a giant foam hand.

I can picture most of the captains in the 1980s and early 1990s who lifted the FA Cup. From Brian Kilcline to Bryan Robson, Alan Hansen to Gary Mabbutt, Steve Perryman to Kevin Ratcliffe, and Steve Bruce to Tony Adams.

It all disappeared when Wembley was demolished.

The sentimentalists regretted the bulldozers moving in and mourned the loss of the stadium's iconic twin towers. The sentimentalists had obviously never tried to go for a wee at the old Wembley, or spent most of a Cup Final watching the game from behind a pillar. It had to go. The stadium needed to change, but so, unfortunately, have trophy presentations.

The demise of the old Wembley coincided with the greater profile of sponsors in the game, and the increasing power of the Champions League. It was no longer enough for a team to go up some steps to pick up a cup, now it needed to be an all-singing, all-dancing event. It didn't matter what the trophy was. The FA Cup, the World Cup, the play-off final for League Two, the Champions League, the Milk-Rumbelows-Worthington-Coca-Cola Cup or whatever, they were all handed over in the same way.

At the final whistle, while one team celebrates and the other collapses tearfully to its collective knees, a swarm of other people dressed in the colours of the competition's sponsors run on to the field carrying bits of plywood and metal. Recruited by the sponsor's PR company, when they applied for their jobs they must have revealed they were quite handy at Lego as children. Their task is to build the stage for the trophy presentation, and they spend around ten minutes trying to put the thing together while the crowd are entertained by the DJ playing some of the hits of the day, or if he can't find them, Tina Turner's 'Simply the Best' on a loop.

Finally, when the stage is built, some official with a clipboard will tell them that it's facing the wrong way. It shouldn't be where the fans can get the best view, it should be where the men and women in the corporate section can get the best view. So the lackeys spend another ten minutes turning the stage round.

The trophy is then carried out on to the pitch, normally by two men with white gloves and surrounded by security guards. I am never sure who they are expecting to try and nick the trophy from the pitch. There would be quite a lot of witnesses. The trophy is then put on a plinth ready for the presentation. Following the trophy on to the stage are normally two fat blokes in suits who look like they've enjoyed a few too many corporate lunches. They are known in the trade as dignitaries, and they will hand out the medals.

The losing team come up first to receive their medals. This is horrible for them, for two reasons: they all have to walk past the trophy that they have failed to win, and they all have to make small talk with Lord Mawhinney, or an equivalent, who wants to talk to them about the game when they just want to get into the dressing room for a shower, and then home to bed.

Then it is the turn of the winners. It is at this point, as a fan, that you wonder who half of these people going up to get medals really are. There are the players who played, the substitutes both used and unused, other members of the first-team squad, other blokes who have suits on and look fit and young so they must be reserve or youth players, the manager, his backroom staff, a couple of directors, a club legend and the ball boys. They all get a medal, and at the back of this conga line of seventy-three people is the captain. He has been stood there hoping that none of his team-mates try to lift the trophy before he gets to it. He winces each time one of them kisses it before him.

Then it is his moment, and as a fan this is your moment as well. The pinnacle of your journey as a supporter is to see your captain lifting a trophy. The players start bouncing around on the stage, which probably isn't wise as they all still have their boots on and the stage looks shiny and slippy. Your captain shakes the hand of the tubby corporate man. His medal is put round his neck. The two of them move towards the plinth. Butterflies are in your stomach at the realization of your club's dream. The captain is grinning. He reaches out for the trophy. It is gleaming. It is yours. Ribbons in your club's colours are draped over it. He has both hands on it. He is ready to cheer. His team-mates are ready to cheer. You are ready to shout and scream and dance with your fellow fans. You have your camera poised as he gets ready to lift it . . .

And then four cannons fire several tons of coloured ticker tape into the air. You can't see a bloody thing. Even the players on the stage can't see more than two feet in front of them, so they don't know whether the cup has been lifted or not. They just keep on bouncing. Meanwhile the captain is half choking to death because he has shouted out 'GET FUCKING IN!' and seven pieces of red and gold ticker tape have gone right down his gullet. All of this is happening while Queen's 'We are the Champions' blares out of the PA system.

As the ticker tape comes to rest and the air clears, the shell-shocked players are ushered off the stage to another area in front of their own fans, who are all looking at their cameras to see if anybody got a shot of anything other than coloured paper. Here, another area has been set up with a big advertising board that carries the name of the sponsor and the trophy that has been won. This is the big moment for the sponsors. This is the shot that the newspapers will use the following morning. The team will be celebrating, spraying champagne over one another, and the sponsor's board will be in front of them on the grass. Except it won't. Two players, who are quite small and worried about getting in the picture if they have to stand with all the big lads at the back, will have lain down in front of the board and put the trophy between them, completely blocking out the sponsor's message. Thank God one of the other players will have been handed a cheap-looking flag saying '[Insert Sponsor Name] congratulates [Insert Team Name] on winning the Cup'.

There follows the lap of honour, where you don't see most of your players because they are being collared by the various international media outlets who are streaming over the pitch for interviews. Then you go home. You reminisce over your photographs taken from so far away you can't make anything out, and if you are a Manchester United fan, you wonder what David May is doing in every single one of them.

THE
FANS

. . . .

Quiet Fans

I feel disingenuous including fans in the book. We are the lifeblood of the game. There is a feeling among footballers and other professionals in the sport that without players and managers, there is no game. They command the six-figure weekly salaries because they are the vital component. It is us, though, who are the vital component. We don't get paid, we don't receive the adulation. It is the opposite, in fact. We pay and we dish out the platitudes, but without us there would be no game. Without us trudging and travelling to game after game, season after season, there would be nobody to watch these players, and, more importantly for them, nothing to pay them with.

Is there camaraderie between us? Is there a common purpose, a feeling that we are all in this together no matter who we support? Is there balls. We are all in our little tribes and we like to moan and slag off one another more than anybody else connected with the game.

One of the best Boxing Days I have ever spent was on the terraces at Boundary Park. Oldham Athletic's ground is not the warmest, even on a balmy day in August, and it was particularly freezing that festive day. I was in the away end for an early kick-off between Oldham and Manchester United. United destroyed the home side, and crucial to their display was Denis Irwin, an unassuming Irish full-back who had cost around £600,000 when Alex Ferguson bought him, from Oldham. We spent most of that day singing 'Thank you very much for Denis Irwin, thank you very much, thank you very very very much' to the tune of the song from the Roses chocolates advert. Simple things, eh? It made us laugh, and as it was Christmas, it seemed strangely appropriate.

I have written elsewhere about the togetherness you feel when you are in the away end and I certainly felt it that day as we all bounced and sang Denis's little ditty together. That spirit, that 'little group of us against a big crowd of them', makes you want to sing, to show your loyalty and make some noise. I hate singing usually. I am tone deaf, can't carry a tune and have no interest in pitch, unless it is a green one to play on. I mime whenever I am required to sing. This is usually at funerals, so I come across as grief-stricken because my mouth is moving but the words just won't come out. I even mimed at my own wedding, although stood at the altar I was actually grief-stricken. Boom boom. So to get me to sing it has to be really special, like appreciating Denis Irwin rather than just something ordinary like getting married. I am thinking this is why I don't sing and bounce at home. And by home I mean at Old Trafford, not in my lounge.

I have been trying to work out why I am quiet for the home matches because you can guarantee that at some stage during the match, or after the match on a phone-in, the away fans will accuse the home fans of being quiet, of there being no atmosphere. I do not care who the home side is, Tottenham or Torquay, Brentford or Birmingham, Crewe or Coventry, the away fans will slag off the home side fans. Even the two most passionate sets of home supporters in the Premier League, at Stoke and at Portsmouth, are not immune from away fans' criticism. To hear the complaints, you would think the home fans are in a library while the away fans are in a disco. That's the image you get. Of course, it's crap. Home fans do make noise, apart from at Arsenal!

It is a complaint that I have never really understood. Are these people who phone television and radio stations to moan about the lack of atmosphere at such and such a ground really that bothered? Why do they not just phone up and say how great their own away support was? It's not really striking a dagger through the heart of the home club to say how quiet their fans were, and it's not exactly an original comment. They are trying to imply that they are proper fans whereas the home support are not true, passionate football fans. In a roundabout way they are accusing them of being middle class. However, there are very obvious reasons why we all accuse the home crowd of being quiet and passionless.

When you are in the away section, you are all tightly bunched together. As I have said elsewhere, you are the hardcore support and you go everywhere with your team. It is easier to get the chants going because you are all close in, you all know the chants, and you need to make some noise because you are outnumbered by the home support.

At Premier League level, when your team is at home I think you become a bit complacent. You expect others to make a noise because there are so many more of you. Also, thanks to the redevelopment of grounds and the building of new stadia, the people who did chant are now scattered all over the place. All the people who used to stand on the Kop, or the North Bank, or the Gwladys Street End are now in different parts of the ground. The collective isn't there any more. There are pockets of fans situated around the grounds who sing and chant but because they aren't in one mass group the noise doesn't sound as intense as it does from the away fans. Home fans do not just sit back and watch the game, they do get involved, just in smaller clusters nowadays.

At Old Trafford, some of the lads who used to stand in the Stretford End in the eighties are now in their late thirties and sit around me in the South Stand. They do their best to get chants going, bless 'em, but it is very hard to do when you are sat to the side of the pitch surrounded by older blokes who would rather watch the football while having a cup of tea and sucking on a Werthers Original. I could join in with them, as I am not at the Werthers Original stage just yet, but I don't. I would feel really self-conscious stood up on my own on my row, with my dad sat next to me wondering what the bloody hell I was doing while the old duffer behind me was trying to get me to sit down. I don't even mime.

I don't think it makes me less of a fan that I don't sing at home. I still cheer, I still clap, I still roar in a slightly em-barrassing way, but circumstances mean I just can't sing. If I was stood up, if I was behind the goal, if I was younger and if it wasn't going to embarrass my dad, then maybe I would. And I think this is the case for the majority of home fans in the Premier League and most home fans in the leagues below, apart from the fact that none of them would worry about showing up my dad.

When Arsenal fans come to Old Trafford, they make a lot of noise, particularly the year they won the title there. The Emirates is quiet, though. Go to the Stadium of Light to watch Sunderland and it isn't exactly bouncing but they sing their hearts out at Anfield. Stamford Bridge has a very corporate feel to it nowadays, but stick the Chelsea fans in the away end at White Hart Lane and they come to life. No club is immune from this state of affairs.

Some clubs have flirted with the idea of having a singing section, which when I first heard about it I thought was a bit twee. I also worried that if you had a singing section and then somebody started a chant and they weren't in the singing section, would they be thrown out? At the same time, if you ended up in the singing section, how much pressure would you be under to deliver quality chants at a loud level? Could you be booted out of the singing section for not performing? Louis Walsh on the pitch at half-time, kicking people out because they didn't have the X Factor while at the same time telling the three lads who were starting every chant that he'd like them to come back to his mansion in Ireland for their own personal boot camp?

Now I am thinking we should have singing sections. And let's be radical and stick them behind one of the goals, and then, as I have advocated elsewhere, stick the away fans behind the other goal. They could chant at each other. There would be more noise and we would be saved those interminable phone-in calls.

Chants

Park, Park, wherever you may be,
You eat dogs in your home country.
It could be worse, you could be Scouse,
Eating rats in your council house.

It is a chant that infuriates the liberal, right-on members of society but it is one of my favourite terrace songs of all time. It is sung to the tune of 'Lord of the Dance', although I never understand why when chants are written down the author has to tell you the tune. Fans can always work out what the tune is just by reading the lyrics.

Ji Sung Park's song is perfect. First and foremost, it is funny. It has a dig at Manchester United's main rivals, Liverpool, and also shows a good knowledge of both geography and global cuisine. It is not essential that a good chant shows knowledge of South Korean delicacies, of course, but it is essential that a good chant has humour.

Fans, throughout my lifetime, have been portrayed in the media as Neanderthal hooligans, always on the lookout for a fight. Throw in the foul language and the odd racist tendency and you have the fan seen through the eyes of *BBC News* during a major tournament, or the *Daily Mail* at any point of the season. Fans are never ever given credit for their wit and humour. Suggest that the songsmiths at our clubs are the Alan Bennetts of the football world and you won't find many people who agree with you.

I liken them to Bennett not just for the wit involved but also the warmth and the self-deprecation. The Park chant shows genuine affection for him, and when players have a chant made for them, it is genuinely because they are loved. Even if they are slightly sarcastic, there is still love for the player in there.

'Don't blame it on Hamann,' the Liverpool fans used to sing to the tune of 'Blame it on the Boogie', 'don't blame it on Biscan, don't blame it on Finnan, blame it on Traore. He just can't, he just can't, he just can't control his feet.' That followed a particularly disastrous FA Cup tie at Burnley when Djimi Traore's spectacularly backheeled own-goal cost them the game. Yes, he's shit, was the Liverpool fans' message, but all we can do is laugh with him, or rather laugh at him.

'When you're sat in row Z and the ball hits your head, that's Zamora' is sung by the Fulham fans at Bobby Zamora. The technical term for his goalscoring record at Craven Cottage up until this season is 'couldn't hit a cow's arse with a banjo', and as much as that frustrates the fans there, his work rate means they find him endearing at the same time.

There are arguments in Scotland over who came up with

CHANTS

'Two Andy Gorams, there's only two Andy Gorams. Two Andy Gorams.' Numerous fans claim to have started singing this shortly after Goram pulled out of a Scotland squad with mental health problems that could have been linked to mild schizophrenia. It could be argued that it sails a little bit close to the wind, that one. The right-on brigade could accuse it of poking fun at mental health, and to be fair, they would have a point. However, does it not show great affection for Goram? I would say it does. Goram had played in goal for many years at Rangers, who aren't exactly liked by fans of other Scottish clubs. At the same time he was the national keeper and won over forty caps for his country. Opposition fans were having a little dig, but I would also like to think that it showed they were thinking of him. In health, if not in football, they were on his side.

A caring, sharing side to football fans? Surely not. But we have got more caring and sharing over the years I have been going to games. Minute silences in the 1980s were never ever silent, and it wasn't just the odd bloke disrupting them, there were massive blocks of noise while others were trying to show their respect. This happened everywhere; no club or group of fans can be absolved. The lack of respect was frightening. It was the same into the nineties. It is only in the last ten or fifteen years that minute silences have started to be properly respected. They have also introduced the minute applause to replace the silence in some cases. It is a method that has been used on the continent, and the reason for bringing it here, we are told, is that it allows the fans to show affection for and appreciation of the person in question.

151

It is a celebration of that person's life rather than a quiet reflection. The other advantage it has is that it is quite difficult to disrupt and disrespect a minute applause. You can shout out during a silence to make a point, or more accurately to just be a twat, but you can't do that when thousands of people are clapping their hands. What are you going to do to disrupt it? Not clap? Not many people are really going to notice that, are they?

So, there is now more humour in the stands, there is more respect when it comes to the silences, there are fewer fights and there is less racism. So why oh why do fans still sing those songs we all know they shouldn't sing?

Non-football-loving people – some do exist, astonishingly – are genuinely surprised that I take a seven-year-old boy to matches. I should clarify that it is my seven-year-old boy, otherwise we could all understand their surprise. Their main problem is the language.

'Doesn't he hear words he shouldn't?' they ask.

'He does,' I reply, 'but I just can't help saying them. They just pop out.'

I don't mind Ben hearing the swearing. He is sport-mad so he isn't going to get through life without hearing swear words, and given that his mother has the mouth of a docker he is likely to use them during his life as well as hear them. I will, however, try and make sure he doesn't swear around his grandparents: his granny can't cope with him saying 'fart', so if he went any stronger she might have a coronary. The swearing is easy to explain to him, less so some of the chants.

When Manchester United have songs as witty as the

Ji Sung Park one, why do fans have to sing songs connecting Arsène Wenger with paedophilia? How do you explain that one to a seven-year-old boy? It is disgusting and a disgrace and actually demeans both the club and the fans. The offenders would tell me that the football ground is not a kindergarten and if you take children then they are in an adult environment and should expect to hear anything. And they would be completely missing the point. That is bollocks, as I would say to Ben. How deep must their hatred of this man be to chant 'sit down you paedophile' at Wenger as he patrols the technical area? It just doesn't have a place in football. It is not funny, neither is it a way of intimidating your opponent or trying to wind him up so he loses his cool in the heat of the battle. It is downright abuse, the sort no human being should have to put up with. It is also slander-ous, though I would imagine it would be a legal minefield to sue thousands of football fans. 'Daddy, what does "bollocks" mean?' is a lot easier to answer than 'Daddy, what's a "paedophile"?' Although the hardest question is 'Daddy, why are they singing about people dying?' I struggle to answer that one.

Hillsborough, Munich, Heysel and Ibrox. Some of the greatest football tragedies of our time with the loss of lives of both players and fans. All of them immortalized, for want of a better word, in song. A quick trawl through message-boards and you will find the hatred and vitriol that leads to these chants still being sung. 'It's all part of the banter between fans' is the common excuse for taking part in these vile songs. People dying is not a subject for banter. Football isn't more important than life and death, whatever Bill Shankly said, and the death of a human being is not the basis for a song, unless you are Elton John.

There is one disaster that I haven't mentioned, that I have never heard sung about. The Bradford City fire. I had family there that day in May 1985 when fifty-six people died in a fire in the all-wood main stand. Fortunately my relatives had chosen not to sit in the main stand that day. I am grateful, for their sakes, that supporters of other clubs do not sing about what happened that day, and at the same time I wonder why not. I can only think that because Bradford City are not a threat to anybody, because they aren't a successful giant of the game like Manchester United, Liverpool or Rangers, there is no jealousy towards them. No hatred.

I have heard Manchester United fans sing about the Hillsborough disaster and not one of them is thinking 'there but for the grace of God'. Do they not realize that if United had not lost their FA Cup quarter-final against Nottingham Forest that year, it could have been United in the semi-final at Hillsborough against Liverpool and it could have been United fans who ended up in the Leppings Lane End? Even if there wasn't a chance that it could have been them, can they not see the pain and the anguish, the sadness and the devastation it caused? Football fans tend to have friends who support other clubs. I have friends who support Liverpool. It could have been them that day in Sheffield. My respect for our friendships is another reason I would never participate in any sick song about their club.

I can't speak and don't want to speak for fans who sing

about Munich or other disasters. I feel the same disgust for them as I feel for the United fans who chant about Hillsborough. When I read about these tragedies or see documentaries on them, it leaves me an emotional wreck. The last thing I would want to do is exploit them. I am not some kind of saint. I am in the majority at games who do not sing about these things. It is the unfortunately vocal minority who give us all a bad name.

This will leave me open to accusations from the hardcore of not understanding the terrace banter, or that I want to make the game more middle class and take it away from its working-class roots. That I am a ponce, or soft and not a real fan. Accuse me of anything you want, but I know I can look in the mirror of a morning and as well as thinking 'Christ, you are looking old and fat', I can also think 'my conscience is clear and I have never sung about the footballing community's dead'. Because, like it or not, no matter who we support, we are all part of the same community.

Tourist Fans

When you are a community, you tend to go one of two ways: you either close up and don't let outsiders into your little gathering or you open your arms and welcome in anybody. You become exclusive or inclusive. Football should be applauded for being as inclusive as possible. It is a sport for all, everybody welcome. But it is difficult to think like that when you get stuck behind some bloody Japanese tourists when you are trying to buy a cup of tea and a programme on your way to your seat. I realize this is unlikely to be a problem if you are a regular at Aldershot, and you will say it serves me right for supporting the club I do, but it gets right on my boy boobs. It may not be a problem for you if you support one of the big clubs either, but I am starting to come to the conclusion that my impatience and my intolerance of non-Mancunian fans at Old Trafford stems from having to live in London.

Until the age of twenty-two I had only ever lived in three cities. Three of the greatest cities on earth, mind you, but three cities that were all distrustful of London. Residents of

Manchester, Paris and Hull are not known for their love of the English capital and friends in all three would tell of their disapproval of a move down south, or in the case of Paris, 'oop North'. 'Oop North', of course, being the French for 'to the north'.

This attitude was based on a lack of friendliness in London, and if you have ever lived in Paris, you will appreciate the irony. The cockneys – because all Londoners are cockneys if you are from the North – were unfriendly, rude, impatient, ignorant, flash, and couldn't say 'bath' or 'grass' properly. I probably haven't written and won't write a sentence in the book with more stereotypes in it than that one, and not many of them – well, not all of them – are true.

They are not all flash.

It is not people from London who are unfriendly or unhelpful, it is people who live in London, and they come from all over the globe to live in the capital. As time goes by, the place reduces you to surliness. The sheer volume of people everywhere leads to you feeling trapped, and as it takes ten minutes to travel one hundred yards by car or a tenner to travel one hundred yards by public transport, you are permanently chasing your tail and frequently in a foul mood. People asking for directions are barked at or, worse, ignored. Pedestrians travelling at less than five miles an hour are barged out of the way or tut-tutted at, and if you think that knife crime is the worst crime affecting London then you ought to ask the people who have the misfortune not to understand escalator etiquette and stand on the left. The left, as any self-respecting capital dweller knows, is for people to hurtle down at breakneck speed while knocking the bags out of the hands of innocent people standing on the right who are minding their own business. It won't be long before the 772 free London newspapers club together to start a campaign to jail those standing on the left, along with all the other serious criminals like drug dealers and murderers.

This sheer feeling of helplessness and the world closing in around you that you experience as you live in London is akin to matchday at Old Trafford. Twenty-five years ago, I would go to the game with forty thousand others. I would hold my dad's hand and be guided through the crowds by him. There was never a problem finding a gap, there was never a problem barging into somebody, there was never a problem nipping into the club shop (Megastores hadn't been invented) to buy a badge or a rosette. I am fairly sure they don't stock rosettes any more.

The counter to this argument is twofold. I was a small boy at that stage and lighter on my feet. Now, at 6'2" and fourteen stone, it is harder to find those gaps, and anybody who has watched me play the sport knows I am not that nimble. The second point is this: whereas it was forty thousand in the eighties, you are talking about seventy-five thousand now. Even the simplest of mathematicians can work out that that is nearly double.

The increase in numbers has brought an increase in the tourist fans. There are Japanese, Koreans, Danish, Swedish, Norwegian, Irish and people from Surrey everywhere, plus hundreds of men and women dressed in 'smart casual' on their way to enjoy a lovely buffet in the corporate seats before the game starts. And not one of all that lot ever seems to have a bloody clue where they are going, and every single one of them has a camera. By the time I get to my seat, having given several sets of directions – wrong ones always to the corporate brigade because they deserve it – and walked straight through several photos by accident, I am as angry as a London commuter in rush hour.

You try not to let your mood affect you, but it does. All of the above isn't just a Manchester United phenomenon, it affects a lot of the major clubs. Several Premier League managers have complained over the past five years of the atmosphere at games changing. In the past, they would argue, fans would get behind the team, whatever the situation. They were there to back not barrack the team. Supporters now have less patience; they are more likely to moan and criticize and, in the case of some, boo. Managers will claim there is a lack of knowledge in modern-day fans. They will blame the curse of the modern society, which demands immediate success and the need for entertainment. But none of them is the main reason. Most fans moan nowadays because they are in a foul mood by the time they sit down because it is such a bloody faff and trial actually to get to your seat.

I am not excusing fans who moan or boo. It would be nice if fans got behind their sides rather than the opposite, and Roy Keane's argument about the 'prawn sandwich' brigade holds true. They are less knowledgeable, they do sit back and expect to be entertained as if they were at the theatre, and they wouldn't know a chant if it hit them in the face. An aria they would be perfectly comfortable with. But there are fans who do need to know the meaning of patience, and who also look on ninety minutes of watching football as a chance to abuse the multi-millionaire privileged members of society that Premier League footballers are.

In the first game of the 2009/10 season, Manchester United were at home to Birmingham City. They had sold Cristiano Ronaldo in the summer and replaced him with Wigan's Antonio Valencia. Valencia had cost £17 million, and for that money, according to the three 'fans' behind me, he had to deliver straight away. He struggled. Genuine fans, genuine Mancunian fans, will give a new player time. Not the three behind me, who spent the whole game slagging him. For that transfer fee, and more importantly because he is probably on around fifty grand a week, he should be a world beater from the word go.

Bemoaning the lack of genuine fans at games and whinge-ing about the number of non-local supporters on matchday makes me sound like a bitter representative of the Republic of Mancunia. And I am. I can't hide it. At the same time I am open to accusations of hypocrisy because my little boy was born in a London suburb. At the moment he is a cockney Red. Hypocritical? Me? Definitely! Desperately wishing I could get him back to Manchester, so he can start swagger-ing like Liam Gallagher and realizing that 'pass' doesn't have an 'r' in it? Definitely.

Accent is quite a big thing outside football grounds. Tele-vision stations now have cameras outside all grounds on matchday and a lot of the grounds on non-matchdays in case a story breaks. If it does, they want to be there so that they can record vox pops. Vox pops are where they stick the camera in the faces of various fans and an anonymous reporter asks for their views on a specific subject. When they do this with the big teams, if they can find fans with accents that bear no resemblance to the area the club is in, then so much the better. It is rare indeed to hear fans outside Anfield, Old Trafford, the Emirates and Stamford Bridge with accents local to the stadia. It all helps to perpetuate the myth that fans of the so-called big four are glory hunters.

There is one club, though, where the fans interviewed always speak with the correct local accent. According to every type of media, these are the best fans in the world ever. They are untouchable and beyond criticism. Loveable, loyal and invariably topless. Bring on the Toon Army.

Newcastle Fans

As the 2008/09 season drew to a close, Newcastle United were fighting for their Premier League lives. The season had been one of complete and utter chaos, and complete and utter mismanagement. Mike Ashley's ownership of the club had been shambolic. Kevin Keegan had come and gone, again, following disagreements with the club's technical director, Dennis Wise (when a club resorts to Dennis Wise as a technical director you know there are problems). Joe Kinnear had come and gone because of ill health, Chris Hughton seemed to be in temporary charge of the team in at least five separate spells, and finally Alan Shearer was given eight games to save the club and keep them in the top flight. He failed.

Not a week went by during this calamitous season when somebody didn't say or write that 'the amazing Newcastle fans' deserved better. Of course they deserved better. Who wouldn't deserve better than that shambles? There isn't one group of supporters of any club in this country you could say deserved that. The implication in this media love-in with the Toon Army is that they are somehow more special than other fans, that in essence they are more loyal.

I spent six months in the summer of 1997 living in the North-East. I worked as a cricket reporter and stayed in a little village called No Place. It could confuse some taxi drivers when at the end of a night out you asked them to take you back to No Place. And I used plenty of taxis to get home after nights out in Newcastle. I had been told before moving there that I would not experience a night out anywhere like a night out in Newcastle. I was sceptical. How different is a night out in one major northern city to one in another northern city? I take Liverpool out of the equation here because I try to wear a hoodie and rarely speak on a night out there for fear of being recognized as a Manc and beaten up. But I was wrong. A night out in Newcastle is like no other. It feels like the whole of the region is out on a Friday and Saturday night. Every place was rammed, the atmosphere was fantastic, and the flesh on display was a joy to behold, even if a lot of it had a slightly orange hue. I loved every single minute of it, and it is a very special place to enjoy yourself. But Newcastle fans more special than other clubs? I don't think so.

The media love-in with Newcastle began with the arrival of Kevin Keegan as manager in 1992. He took them from the bottom of the second tier of English football and into the Premier League. The football was free-flowing, the goals flew in and they were in with chances of winning the title. They were referred to as 'everybody's second favourite team'. If anything is going to wind up football fans, it is a suggestion that they might like another team as well as their own. It questions their loyalty. At the same time it makes the Newcastle fans even more loyal because their team is also their second favourite team. That's how special they are.

Once they became 'everybody's second favourite team' in the media, they actually became everybody's favourite club to question about the loyalty of their fans. As commentators spoke about the amazing atmosphere at St James's Park and their love for the team, the players, the club and Keegan, other fans were scouring the record books to find proof of the Newcastle fans' disloyalty. No club's attendance record has been more debated and argued about.

St James's Park might have been packed to the rafters when Philippe Albert chipped Peter Schmeichel to make it 5–0 but they only averaged 16,860 in the 1990/91 season when they were at the bottom of Division Two. Thousands might have come out to welcome Alan Shearer when he signed for the club but only 21,033 were watching them when Kevin Keegan took over the club. Then, to really ram it home, as the argument rages on, somebody who thinks he is being original but is in fact just a cliché will quote Manchester City's average attendance when they dropped into the third tier for a season in 1998/99. It was 28,273, if you are interested.

This amusing stat-fest leads you to some hysterical arguments on the interweb. The toonarama website was invaluable for this little section, providing all of Newcastle's attendance figures since 1946/47, with graphs and division stats as well. For the record, in fifty-three of the sixty-three seasons they report on, Newcastle's average was higher than the top-flight average. And the comparisons with Manchester City obviously hurt, because on the nufc.com site there is a whole section devoted to City's attendances. 'If you get in an argument with a City fan,' it advises, 'remind them that on the 5th December 1998 when they hosted Mansfield, the crowd was 3,007 (658 away fans).' That will show 'em. It will show 'em you are a stat-obsessed geek who has probably never kissed a girl. If you then go on to a City site, you will find them worrying. They are rightly proud of their fans' loyalty when they were in Division Two, but now they are concerned that Leeds fans might be considered more loyal if their average is higher now they are in the equivalent, League One.

Not that loyalty can be measured by attendance figures alone. The TV companies' love of sticking Geordies on camera at any given opportunity has led to other disturbing tendencies. Fans were never seen crying until Newcastle blew their head-to-head title race with Manchester United. All of a sudden there were men, women and children in black and white crying their eyes out. That is how much they cared. They cared enough to cry. So now, if you don't cry, you don't care. The cameras search out tearful fans. Lose the FA Cup Final – get that kid in tears. Lose the final match of the season to get relegated – look, there are two grown men sobbing, focus on them. Lose at Stoke on a cold Tuesday night in a meaningless game – what do you mean nobody has a tear in their eye? They must do. Somebody has to cry whenever their team loses. Showing fans in tears has now become as dull as always seeing footage of that curly-haired nobhead Arsenal fan celebrating them winning the league at Old Trafford, *every time* Manchester United host Arsenal. Having said all of that, I would always rather see blubbing fans than blubber fans.

The final test of loyalty we all now have to go through thanks to the Toon Army is the fat topless test. If you don't have several blokes over twenty stone who are prepared to stand in the away end with their shirts off for the whole ninety minutes of a football match, then you are not a proper set of fans. You are not genuine. You cannot be loyal if you don't have grown men prepared to freeze their not inconsiderable tits off for their club.

Where did this trend come from? Why are they always fat? I can't answer the first one, but the second question I can have a stab at. You don't see thin people doing this because they would die of hypothermia if they tried it. The fatties do have several layers of flab to keep the chill off. Being topless isn't enough, though: several tattoos are required on the upper body, all connected to the team. If the club crest can be tattooed in the stomach area, so that the belly button is incorporated into it, then you get extra bonus points.

The media's obsession with Newcastle's fans over the last fifteen years has turned them into an easy subject of ridicule for other fans. As we have seen, it has led to arguments over attendances, more tears shed than at the end of *Bambi*, and more man boobs on show than any right-minded person wants to see. It has led to Noel Gallagher stating 'There's no better sight than seeing fat topless Geordies crying.' Fans of other clubs demonize them because the media idolize them. Blackpool fans are just as loyal, as are Burton fans, as are Everton fans. They might not be as numerous, but they are as loyal. No club's fans deserve bad things to happen to them, no set of fans is more special than another set. We all suffer, we all dream, we all enjoy, we all wish we were playing. We are all fans. We are all needed by the game. We all deserve respect. We are all lucky. We are all special.

That's all the nice, warm, sentimental stuff dealt with. Now on to a group of people I just can't defend.

The England Band

A couple of years ago I decided to run the London Marathon. It was a pretty naive decision, taken without any inkling of just how much pain I was letting myself in for. When you run the marathon, the organizers lay on entertainment along the route to help you on your way, although why a man juggling outside an East End boozer should motivate you to run twenty-six miles is anybody's guess. I was particularly struck by the number of steel bands that popped up along the route. Actually, I found these to be quite useful, because as soon as the sound of them banging their drums reached my ears, it forced me to speed up until I was far enough past them to no longer hear the racket. I had to do this several times during the race and I'm incredibly grateful to each and every one of them for helping me break five hours.

It's not that I mind steel bands, but there is a time and a place for them. On a beach in Antigua perhaps, while lounging in the sun. Not under a flyover in Rotherhithe. It is the same with a brass band. I do not mind listening to them in a concert hall or at a village fête, but I do not expect them to be sat three rows behind me at an international football match. Who in their right mind ever thought that it would be a good idea to stick a few blokes with trumpets and another bloke with a big drum in among the England supporters? Who in their right mind ever thought that the England Supporters Band would be liked?

I don't know a great deal about this bunch of 'musicians', apart from the fact that they get right on my tits. I did think about Googling them, but I would rather have 'transvestites + donkeys' on my internet history than 'the England band'. In my limited knowledge of them, they are loosely connected with Sheffield Wednesday, although rumour has it that the fans of the club don't particularly like that association. My first encounter with them was at Euro 2000, and since then they have ruined every single England match for me.

Football fans don't need a band to help them sing songs. Virtually all the supporters of Premier League and Football League clubs manage to chant perfectly happily without any musical accompaniment. Portsmouth have a bloke who rings a bell, but that's because he's a bit mad, and a lot of Spanish clubs have a fat bloke with a big drum, but that's because they are Spanish. Here in Britain, fans have always relied on their natural tunefulness to get them through the songs.

Maybe the songs at international level are more complicated than at club level, so the singing of songs mirrors the football itself. Or maybe, when it comes to representing your country on the terraces, it's a step up in class and that's why the band are there, to help us all through the more difficult songs.

It would be nice to think that was the case. Except it isn't. The band don't exactly have a great repertoire. They do the National Anthem, they do 'Rule Britannia', and more than anything else they do The Bloody Great Bloody Escape. Everyone knows the tune to that. We don't need a band to help us. And it's not as if the lyrics are complicated. For those of you who don't know them, they are as follows:

Der der, der der de der der, der der de der de der de der der.
Der der, der der de der der, der der de der der de der.
England!

And repeat until you want to smash the trumpet player senseless with his instrument.

It was at the 2002 World Cup in South Korea and Japan that I discovered something that shocked me – that the world's most annoying band since The Lighthouse Family were supported by the English football authorities. And not just supported, they were in fact positively encouraged by them. A group of faceless suits who had never sat among proper fans in their lives were actually giving this lot free tickets to all England games, home and away, so that they could 'help the atmosphere'. Jesus H. Christ. This, however, did explain a couple of things that had been troubling me. How did they manage to always sit together? Whenever I booked for a group of us to go to a game, one of us always ended up in a different part of the stadium. So why did the bloke with the big drum never end up in the away end by accident? Now I knew. It also explained how they managed to get their instruments into every game. I would always get asked to leave my bottle of water at the body search because it could be construed as a weapon. Yet the Louis Armstrong of the England band was allowed to take his cornet in with him. If you were a player taking a corner, what would you rather hit you on the bonce, a plastic bottle or part of the brass section of an orchestra? I'm tempted to tell the FA that I'm not half bad on the triangle and see if it gets me free entry to international matches for the next ten years.

So this is a plea to the person who makes decisions on these things, probably a man at the FA called the 'England Band liaison officer'. Please, let's disband the England band. Allow the genuine supporters to come up with some new tunes and lyrics. Free up some extra tickets by not giving them to the band for every game, and allow us all to enjoy England matches again without having someone blowing a trumpet in our ears. If I wanted to spend two hours listening to that, I'd rent out *Brassed Off* on DVD.

THE
MANAGER

....

Owners and Directors

The gaffer. The boss. The guvnor. The ultimate job in foot-ball – to be the master of all he surveys, the man in control of a kingdom. Well, he is meant to be the master of all he surveys. At a lot of clubs over the past few years there have been many managers who haven't felt in control of every-thing, thanks to the rise of the roles commonly known as the 'Director of Football' and 'the interfering foreign owner'.

You cannot look back through the decades at the role of the football club owner with rose-tinted glasses. There have always been plenty of arrogant, self-obsessed men who used football clubs as extensions of their own egos. The obligatory rule when writing on this subject is that you have to mention Len Shackleton. In his autobiography, the Sunderland legend included a chapter headed 'The Average Director's Know-ledge of Football'. As you are no doubt aware, the page was empty and the footnote at the bottom read 'This chapter has deliberately been left blank in accordance with the author's wishes.'

And in among Brian Clough's gems is this one: 'Football

hooligans? Well, there are ninety-two club chairmen for a start.'

My memories of 1980s club chairmen are dominated by one man: Robert Maxwell, the newspaper proprietor who controlled Oxford United and then Derby County. He was always the subject of films on *Football Focus* and the like, to the extent that I would struggle to name another football club chairman from that decade bar Martin Edwards at Manchester United, and at one stage Edwards was going to sell the club to Maxwell. Maxwell's business practices were dodgy to say the least and Oxford United suffered as a result. Then in 1991 Maxwell fell off his boat and died.

Maxwell, you could argue, was one of the first foreign owners in this country, having been born in Czechoslovakia. He escaped to Britain in 1940 to flee the Nazis and settled on his English moniker a few years later. So maybe Maxwell was ahead of his time, although those who invested in his pension funds are unlikely to agree. Now the national game is awash with foreign owners. We have Americans, Middle Eastern businessmen, Russians and other Eastern Europeans in charge of our football clubs.

Some, like Randy Lerner at Aston Villa, run their clubs like businesses and let their managers get on with the job, taking a back seat themselves. Others treat their clubs as their plaything and enjoy interfering at every level. Then there are some who saddle the clubs they have taken over with a massive amount of debt and do everything they possibly can to avoid being questioned on the subject. How did these kind of men rise to the top in business while being so reclusive? This last subject is far too serious and far too complex for a book like this, although their practices and methods make me worry for the game's future. For this chapter, it is the owners who use their clubs as toys who interest me.

They have the money to buy anything they want, and that means they have the money never to be refused anything. Money brings power, and power means control. Herein lies the problem. The owner shouldn't be in control of the football club, the manager should be. The manager wants to run things from top to bottom, overseeing not just the first team but transfers, coaching, scouting and the youth set-up, to name just some. These owners are averse to this. If they want one of the world's best players at their club, they will try and buy him, regardless of whether or not he'll fit into the system the manager likes to play, and even if he's known for having a disruptive influence wherever he goes. A manager will have a certain way of playing. He has found it to be successful and it has brought results. The owner may decide it is not pleasing on the eye. He wants his side to be the footballing equivalent of the Harlem Globetrotters and wants to bring in players to achieve that aim, immediately.

I have been told of one owner who stood in the tunnel ahead of his club's first game of the season. They were at home, and it was a typical opening-day-of-the-season afternoon. The sun was shining, the fans were in their new shirts – more than likely saying to one another how good the pitch looked (because that is always the first topic of conversation on the opening day) – and there was enthusiasm in the air. There wasn't enthusiasm in the tunnel. The owner was explaining to a friend from another sport that his team were shit. The players brought in were shit. The players who had stayed were shit. Everything was shit.

'And who is this team we are playing anyhow?'

'They are . . . they are . . .' the owner continued, struggling to remember the opponents. 'Who are they?' he asked a member of the coaching staff. When told, his response was 'Are they in our league?', thereby showing an amazing grasp of how English football and the first day of the season works. I can't remember one single opening day when a team didn't play another team in the same division.

As the football club becomes a status symbol for the foreign businessman, so the homegrown version starts to get interested. Clubs owned by generations of the same family are disappearing as British tycoons try to keep up with the wealthy foreigners. And several of them are as clueless and as interfering as their overseas counterparts. A friend of mine was in a business meeting with a club chairman not so long ago. This chairman has several other companies as well as a football club. As the meeting dragged on, my friend asked the man what he was writing down because he was obviously paying no attention to what was going on. 'Saturday's starting eleven,' was the reply. He was going to leave that meeting, phone his manager and tell him what the line-up should be at the weekend.

Is it any wonder, then, in this climate of uncertainty, egotistical owners and the immediate need for success, that a lot of managers come across as incredibly grumpy buggers?

Press Conferences

I have been massively fortunate to present a lot of football programmes on both television and radio, and it is a privilege. The biggest thrill I get from hosting these shows is meeting people within the game, and managers in particular. The art of managing fascinates me. I am one of those people addicted to *Championship Manager* or *Football Manager* who genuinely believes that because I have won the Champions League with Dagenham and Redbridge on a computer screen I could do the same thing in real life. That is, until I meet and talk to the real deal.

David Moyes, Roy Hodgson, Gordon Strachan, Alan Curbishley, Harry Redknapp and Graham Taylor are all managers I have worked with and whose company I have enjoyed immensely. After working with each of them I have phoned up a mate or my dad and not far off swooned over them. I have described every single one of them at some point as the 'nicest man in football'. And at the time I was with them that's genuinely what they were.

I cold-called Harry Redknapp once and left a message on

his mobile. Within ten minutes he had returned my call and we were chatting for a good half hour. It is not that remarkable a story, unless you work in football and you understand how difficult it is to get anybody to return your call, let alone talk to you.

David Moyes was once a studio pundit for a UEFA Cup game I was presenting. He talked me through the whole game tactically, explaining in detail what each side would try to do as well as telling me afterwards of his love for Russian football and players to look out for. It was an education, and an enjoyable one. Roy Hodgson imparted his incredible knowledge of the game in general and Italian football in particular when I worked on Serie A and was a perfect gentleman, as is Graham Taylor, a man I have so much time for because he is generous with his time and his thoughts and displays no trace of bitterness despite everything he went through as England manager. We have spoken many times about his 'turnip' treatment and despite his honesty in discussing it, I can still see the sadness in his eyes. As a nation we should feel immensely guilty for how we treated a man who was doing his dream job and trying to do his best with no luck.

I hope to God that you don't think I am name-dropping here. I am merely trying to point out that all of these men have always spoken to me with eloquence and intelligence. I do not doubt as well that a lot of the others in their profession would do the same, so it begs the question, what the hell happens to them when they enter a press conference or have to do a pre- or post-match interview? It is often like pulling teeth with a surly teenager. How do these men, who can be so relaxed and happy to talk in the right environment, turn into yes/no merchants who refuse to take questions on certain subjects? Is it our fault, as in the media? Is it the fans' fault for constantly wanting access to and accountability from their managers? Or is it the situations that these interviews take place in? It is probably a mixture of all three.

At media conferences now you haven't just got three blokes and a dog, these are events that need to be managed carefully. There are radio and television stations, there are websites, and there are newspapers. But you can't just lump all the papers together. They have to be separated into the local papers, the daily papers and the Sunday papers. Everybody has their own demands and everybody has their own agendas. The Sunday papers need a different angle to a story from the dailies. Some of the electronic media might be from a different country wanting to know about one of their compatriots' current form or fitness. The TV and radio stations need to get something out of the conference immediately so that they can run with it straight away and be ahead of the written media.

It is a bun fight, and in the eye of the storm (I think I am mixing my metaphors) is the manager. The stuff you see on the telly or hear on the radio is only a small part of it. The manager will do one big general conference and then more often than not have separate briefings with the papers (one for the locals, one for the dailies and one for the Sundays), and then maybe some 'one on ones', sit-down interviews with just one journalist from a television or radio station.

The poor sods have to spend a long time doing this, nearly every single week, so is it any wonder they appear a little pissed off and monosyllabic?

My sympathies aren't all with the managers, though. You hear how in years gone by journalists were mates with managers. They would share twelve pints of mild and twenty-seven woodbines and still have change for a chippy tea between the two of them as they jumped on the bus home. A relationship would be built, trust would be earned, and all parties would benefit. Sit in a press conference now and trust is not something that is in the air. Hostility? Most definitely. Suspicion? Without a doubt. Superiority? Certainly. It is a them-and-us situation.

With hackles raised, then, the atmosphere is invariably tense, and it makes asking questions tricky and occasionally nerve-racking. Ask anything controversial and the wrath of the man sitting behind the microphones is likely to be unleashed on you as colleagues watch on, thanking the Lord it wasn't them.

'What do you make of your next opponents?'

'Tell us how well you think [insert name of player who is at the top of his game] is playing.'

'Could you tell us why you are so great?'

'Aren't your fans like a twelfth man at home?'

'What's your favourite colour?'

These are all questions that are suitably bland and sycophantic and usually answered with no problem whatsoever. But head into this kind of territory . . .

'You always struggle against these opponents. Why?'

'Why is [insert name of player who couldn't trap a bag of cement or hit a barn door] playing so badly?'

'Why have you and the owner fallen out?'

... and just watch as the man before you turns puce, steam comes out his ears and the press officer next to him tut-tuts and shakes his or her head at you.

Nothing humorous comes out of these encounters any more. Any internet search of football quotes will unearth pearls from Clough (he appears frequently in this chapter), Shankly, Stein, Atkinson (before he had his little bit of trouble), Venables, Allison and Robson that will have you laughing out loud. It is a struggle to find quotes from managers over the last decade that will even make you smile, let alone laugh. Humour is as rare as anger is all too common.

The anger is all part and parcel of these occasions, but it is nowhere near as bad as the feeling of being patronized.

Football is a tactical game. It might make me sound like a geek but I love that side of the game and working out the positives and negatives of various formations. If I ever ask you one night if you fancy a drink, it is probably in your best interests to turn me down to avoid being bored to death. I would love to ask Alex Ferguson about the benefits of playing Wayne Rooney out on the left, as he did a lot in the 2007/08 and 2008/09 seasons. I think it is because he can cut infield from that position to leave more room for Patrice Evra to get into attacking positions, for what it is worth. Equally it would be worth hearing Carlo Ancelotti's thoughts on the benefits of playing a midfield diamond system, or Rafa Benitez's feelings on why he uses Steven Gerrard in a position just behind Fernando Torres rather than in a central midfield position.

I did tell you to avoid a night out with me. Hope you are still awake.

The problem is, when you ask a serious football question that could be tactical, the response you get is never particularly favourable. I am not singling out the three managers above, it could be any of them, but you'll get a look that suggests 'Who are *you* to be talking to *me* about tactics?' The inference is that they are the professionals, working in the game, and you are making a living off the back of them, so what do you know about tactics? I might know very little but I would like to learn more by asking these kinds of questions and getting some decent answers. Rather than interesting, informative responses coming out of these events, they instead turn into one massive lump of blandness, everybody just going through the motions because that's just how these conferences are, how they are run.

It is truly a tough call, though, whether the press conference is worse than the pre- and post-match tunnel interviews.

Pre- and Post-Match Interviews

There are few people in football who elicit more sympathy from me than the match reporters, the poor men and women who spend a huge proportion of their lives in the dark recesses of football stadia interviewing grumpy men in front of advertising boards for loads of products you have never heard of. Whatever the weather, whatever the game, whatever the situation, they are expected to shove a microphone under the nose of an interviewee to gain an insight into the game we are about to watch, or have just watched. They have to be a cross between Jeremy Paxman and a counsellor. They have to get the questions right while at the same time judging the mood of the interviewee to make sure they don't upset him. It is a thankless task.

It would be made a heck of a lot easier for these poor creatures if their interviewees were in any way accommodating. But they aren't. The football manager goes out of his way to be as obdurate and unhelpful as possible. There are exceptions, who tend to be younger, foreign or Harry Redknapp. The result is an often tedious exchange where the manager tells us nothing and the reporter can't extract anything of value out of them, through no fault of their own.

In May 1996, Kevin Keegan became apoplectic during a post-match interview. Alex Ferguson had made disparaging remarks about some of Newcastle's opponents, and when asked about those comments, Keegan, to use a common term, lost it. With the two-horse title race reaching its finale, he went for the Manchester United manager live on Sky with his now infamous 'I would love it' rant. It is still talked about. It is still discussed. Kevin Keegan will go to his grave with that being one of the most famous moments of his career, which is sad considering he is a former European Footballer of the Year.

It is held up as an example of Alex Ferguson's brilliant mind games, which succeeded, as Manchester United pipped Newcastle to the Premier League title that year. I would hold it up as an example of how crap all other post-match interviews are. We are still talking about it fourteen years on because there hasn't been another memorable conversation with a manager since.

It is also held up as an example of Keegan's weakness in the heat of battle. I would argue that it should be used as an example of Keegan's refreshing honesty and passion. Not for him, media training. Not for him, yes and no answers, and not for him, demands beforehand that he not be asked questions on certain subjects, such as Alex Ferguson's comments. Because those demands also hamper the post- or pre-match interview.

This is the life of the reporter. They are stood in a freezing cold tunnel waiting for their pre-match interview. As a journalist, and the majority are all good journalists, they want to ask the manager about the big story that has affected his club that week, the transfer request put in by one of his star players. The manager arrives for the two-minute interview one minute before he is due to do it, and says he won't talk about his player's transfer request. Simply won't entertain any question on the subject. It leaves the reporter having to ask questions like 'So, you looking forward to the game?' and 'This will be a tough test for you, won't it?' while wanting to ask 'What on earth is going on with this transfer request?' Worse, the viewer is screaming at the telly that the reporter is a nob for not asking the only question they want an answer to.

I have never understood the refusal to even take a question on a subject. These are eloquent, intelligent men. The situation above actually happened with a manager who I have worked with in the past and had full and frank discussions with. He could have handled a question on a transfer request, no problem, yet he chose to make it difficult. I once checked with Gary Neville if there were any questions he wanted to avoid. He said that if there was a question he didn't want to answer he would just tell me during the interview with the words 'I am not answering that'. It's quite simple really.

I have more sympathy with managers in the post-match interview, especially if they have just been beaten. They have a range of emotions running through them – anger and bitterness are both usually in there somewhere – yet they are expected to give a cold and calculated analysis of the game they have just been involved in. They have to keep their temper in check because one word out of place, particularly about the officials, and they could be hit with a touchline ban or a fine. If they are asked about a controversial incident in the game then invariably, if it was their own player or team that was the sinner, they won't have 'seen it'. I think we all know the master of that phrase, don't we?

Often, they arrive for these 'grillings' with more demands on what they will and won't answer. If the reporter ignores those requests, the manager will more than likely wreak his revenge through the particularly childish act of banning the reporter and the station he or she works for.

Media Bans

There are very few sections in this book where you could say ''twas ever thus', which is good, because it's a phrase that makes you sound like a smartarse. However, it really does apply to this part on media bans. Managers and journalists have always fallen out and in the course of arguments and bust-ups the reporters involved have been banished from the club for a period of time. If they haven't been banned then the managers will have a spell when they just won't talk to the journalists concerned and will instruct their players to do the same. Eventually time heals the rift, the problem is forgotten and everybody moves on. In recent years, though, the sheer proliferation of media organizations means it is very difficult to keep up with who is banning who in the modern game, plus some of today's managers have an amazing ability to keep a grudge going for years.

As someone who has been known to have the odd sulk – I may have mentioned already that I have the personality of a stroppy toddler at times – I have a grudging admiration for grudges. They have to be proper grudges, though.

Increasingly, I think managers are looking for the slightest excuse to ban somebody, anybody, simply to reduce their media commitments. Receiving a ban for just giving an opinion or being critical of one aspect of a club or a team is an overreaction. I assumed you had to be tough and thick-skinned to get to the top of the management tree, yet most of them appear to be as sensitive as a tooth hit by a bolt of lightning after a mouthful of ice cream in one of those TV adverts.

It has been known for managers to take such exception to how they have been interviewed after a match that they have demanded a letter of apology from the post-match inter-viewer. I have been told by one of the people who has had to do this that their letter of apology wasn't sincere or apologetic enough so could they try again, please. They refused. Good for them. What a pathetic way to try to assert your power and influence within the game.

It is impossible to keep up with which manager has banned which outlet, and in these days of media empires some people end up getting barred through no fault of their own. One radio station was once banned by a club because the pundit they used had said something critical on a tele-vision channel. A whole station refused access to the club through no fault of their own. A TV station has been barred in the past because of something written in a newspaper. The paper and the TV station were owned by the same media mogul so were lumped in together.

Sports journalists can find themselves out on their ear because of something written by their colleagues in the news section. As footballers and managers have become more attractive targets for celebrity gossip and kiss-and-tells, the sportswriter's world has become a more treacherous place. They can easily be barred because a story has appeared on the front page of their paper about a 'three-way romp on the back seat of a Baby Bentley'. This story is about a footballer, obviously, not the sportswriter. There is no way a sports journalist could afford a Baby Bentley. And actually, when you see most of them, there aren't many women who would want a three-way romp with any of them either. They'd be lucky to get a one-way romp.

The BBC suffer more than most from this conflict of interest, and I am not just saying this because I have spent a large part of my working life in their employment. Because of its size it is very easy for one of its departments to piss somebody off without the rest of the corporation knowing. So before you know it, you can't talk to a certain manager because of something (that you are unaware of) that has been done by someone (you have no idea who) in some pro-gramme (that you have never watched). Over the years they have queued up to ban the Beeb. Harry Redknapp and Sam Allardyce are just two who spring to mind, but the daddy of them all when it comes to refusing to talk to the licence payers is Fergie.

Sir Alex Ferguson's feud with the BBC has been on and off since the turn of this century. He has taken exception to various comments made by the corporation's football experts and has issued his bans accordingly. His latest one, though, has been running since 2004, which is a heck of a long time not to talk to somebody. He was less than impressed with a *Panorama* programme that investigated his son Jason, who was then an agent. I can just imagine the editor of *Match of the Day*, sat at home in dressing gown and slippers, sipping his cocoa as he got ready to watch *Panorama*. As one part of the BBC rarely talks to another, he will have watched the titles roll, seen the subject of the programme that night and then thought, 'Oh shit. Here comes a ban.'

So, because of a news programme, everybody connected with the sporting side has been punished. All the BBC's football programmes on television, Radio Five Live and, most unfortunately, BBC Radio Manchester. It is local radio that really needs relationships with its local clubs to flourish, but thanks to a latte-sipping, drainpipe-wearing journalist (I would imagine with black-rimmed spectacles and a haircut he could get away with if he was fifteen years younger) they are suffering. The rest of us are suffering too because we, the viewers, now have to endure the thoughts of Mike Phelan every Saturday night. Have we not suffered enough, Sir Alex?

When it comes to issuing bans, this long, seemingly never-ending one is not Ferguson's greatest achievement. Oh no. Brilliantly, he has been known to ban his own club's media outlets in the past. On a couple of occasions he has been less than impressed with comments made by either presenters or pundits on MUTV. Whenever he has felt they were too critical, for the subsequent match he has refused pre- and post-match interviews. He wouldn't talk to his *own* club's *own* TV channel! It doesn't give the rest of us much hope, does it, if he's doing that?

After this little section, I am envisaging a long ban myself.

Dress Sense

To Ben and his friends, and to anybody reading this who is under the age of twenty-five, think yourself lucky. You have never had to witness topless, hairy managers wallowing in team baths with champagne, trophies and several women young enough to be their daughters. It was a recurring image as I grew up. Photos of legendary 1970s managers frolicking in various states of undress – it could have scarred me for life.

And if you weren't seeing managers semi-naked in the late seventies and early eighties, you'd see them stood on touch-lines in giant coats and hats wearing the contents of several Christmas crackers on their fingers. Bling wasn't something invented by Jay-Z and Kanye West, let me tell you. It was devised by Malcolm Allison and Ron Atkinson. Christ on a bike. It wouldn't surprise me if they were to reveal on their deathbeds that they ramraided a Ratners every week just to keep themselves in rings and bracelets.

Hats were an important part of the managerial uniform in the seventies and eighties. The aforementioned Allison went for a fedora, others had trilbies, and even into the nineties Alan Ball's headgear of choice was a flat cap. It made him look like someone who had been on a nice country walk through Emmerdale, taken a wrong turning and ended up on the bench at Maine Road.

Headgear has largely disappeared in this millennium, although you do still get the odd manager wearing a cap. Tony Pulis at Stoke City is one. I'm not sure if he is wearing it as a sponsor's requirement like a Formula One racing driver, or for a bet, but I wish he wouldn't because baseball caps do look particularly embarrassing on anybody over the age of thirty. I suppose we should be grateful he isn't wearing it backwards to really get down with the kids.

The plethora of jewellery has also disappeared. It is extremely difficult to work a tactics board or stand on the touchline waving your hands about to give the impression you are handing out important tactical instructions if your digits are weighed down by half a ton of Ernest Jones's finest. And we should thank our lucky stars that the men in charge of our football teams no longer look like a cross between Del Boy and a pimp.

That is not to say that they are immune from criticism, though. Well, not criticism. Piss-taking would be a better description.

The modern-day manager has two options available to him when choosing his matchday attire. Leisurewear or businesswear. Tracksuit chav or Armani model. It's a tricky choice.

Martin O'Neill leads the way for managers adopting the

tracksuit look. He has been described as the new Brian Clough for his managerial style. He is intelligent and quirky and can be a little off the wall – very similar, therefore, to the man he played under at Nottingham Forest. It is his clothing style that reminds me of Old Big 'Ead as well. Green jumper and tracksuit bottoms every time for Clough. Jumper and tracksuit bottoms for O'Neill.

The colour doesn't matter for O'Neill, but it did matter for Owen Coyle. While he was Burnley manager he always wore a bright white jumper when on the bench that made him look like he was in a Daz advert. I half expected to find Danny Baker and Shane Ritchie as his assistants. It was absolutely pristine before every game. Paul Hart, Pulis and Mick McCarthy are others who go for the shellsuited bottoms, like a Harry Enfield scouser, with a nice comfy jumper on top.

I can imagine you are now thinking that I really ought to get out more and not pay quite so much attention to the dress sense of our top managers. But I haven't finished. Let's now examine the businesswear look!

Most managers now like to wear a well-cut suit on the touchline. In deep midwinter they will team this with an official club coat. This will have their initials on so we do not forget who they are or what they are called. Either that or they work at a club with a history of kit going missing so it is important that everybody's kit is labelled correctly. Honestly, the number of times Ryan Giggs has accidentally gone home with Alex Ferguson's coat in his kit bag, only for his mum to tut, tell him to be more careful, wash it and then send it back in with him on the Monday morning.

The suit gives the manager an air of authority. It shows everybody who is in charge and can make them look like a catwalk model (although this is more appropriate when describing José Mourinho than when describing Sam Allardyce). But as more bosses adopt the suited and booted look, I have noticed something rather disturbing about them. This doesn't apply to the older managers around, the Fergusons, the Wengers, the Ancelottis. This applies more to those who are in their thirties and forties.

As many of us will be aware, it is difficult to get your clothing right at this stage of your life. I have found it difficult to get my clothing right at any stage of my life, but it feels particularly hard in my mid-thirties with my forties looming ever closer and ever quicker. It would be embarrassing to be still trying to be cool with my outfits, trying to wear 'what's in' but just ending up looking like a very fat, very aged eighteen-year-old. At the same time, though, I don't want to start dressing like my dad, fashionista though he is. You feel caught between a rock and a hard place. Or rather, you feel caught between Topman and Austin Reed.

Football managers in this age range are no different. What I have noticed them doing is trying to dress like their players, but doing it eighteen months after them. The players start wearing ties with big fat knots in them, eighteen months later some of the managers have big fat knots. The players then start wearing jumpers under their suit jackets, eighteen months later the managers start wearing jumpers under their suit jackets. Gareth Southgate actually combines the big fat knot look and the jumper look. The players have now started to wear skinny ties, so give it a year or so and the managers will ditch the fat knots and the jumpers and start digging out the ties they last wore in 1986 while dancing to Duran Duran.

We must thank our lucky stars that they haven't copied the players' tendency to wear oversized headphones. I don't think I could bear to watch an interview with Phil Brown with some dubstep bleeding out of the great big white cans around his neck. I know, I know. I have gone too far with that last analogy. As if Phil Brown would be so ridiculous as to wear headphones during a game. Headsets, on the other hand . . .

Headsets

When you watch a game of American football, as well as giving up five hours of your life, you notice that every single member of the coaching team is wearing a headset. There are various reasons for this. There are 135 of them for a start, some of them sat three miles away from the guys on the touchline, up in the stands, and the game is incredibly tactical with hundreds of plays, both offence and deeeee-eeeeeeefence, planned for each match, so communication between them all is important. None of these factors applies to a game involving Bolton Wanderers or Blackburn Rovers. Which begs the question, why did Big Sam start wearing a headset?

Big Sam is, of course, Sam Allardyce. I think it is important at this stage to give you a little bit more information on him. Allardyce was born in 1954 in the West Midlands. His playing career as a big, no-nonsense centre-half took in Bolton, Sunderland and Huddersfield, to name but three. His managerial career started at Blackpool and Notts County before he arrived at Bolton in 1999, where he stayed

199

for the next eight years. It is a career and a background that could be described as old school. I mean nothing derogatory by that, but others, particularly in the media, could use 'old school' as an insult.

At Bolton, Allardyce was one of the most forward-thinking managers in the Premier League. His team may not have played total football, but they were effective, and his methods off the pitch were innovative. He rescued the careers of some ageing footballers such as Ivan Campo, Youri Djorkaeff and Jay Jay Okocha. He made them fitter, less injury-prone, and gave them a new lease of life. Yet because his side were direct and he was a 6'3" former centre-half from the West Midlands who had managed in various northern outposts he was still seen by some, harshly so, as a gruff and basic manager. So, what better way to show the world that you aren't like that, that in fact you are forward-thinking and progressive?

Wear a headset. That's what.

It immediately shows that you are at the forefront of modern technology. It shows that you are thinking about ways to innovate. It shows that you are following the example of coaches in other sports so you are thinking about your trade. It shows that you are using your coaching team as extra eyes and ears in the stadium, that you are a team and that you are not a dictator. It shows that you are taking advice from others. It shows that you are taking manage-ment to the next level.

Of course, it only shows all of that if it is actually switched on and there are other members of your coaching staff in the stands using theirs. With Big Sam, that did appear to be the case. It did seem that other members of his management team were in the stands at the Reebok feeding stuff into his ears. With others, I am not too sure.

Phil Brown and Sammy Lee were both part of Big Sam's backroom staff and both went on to manage and adopt the headset look. Little Sam's headset was a little black number with a massive earpiece just like Big Sam's. Brown, on the other hand, has chosen to wear a flesh-coloured earpiece and microphone on the touchline. That is flesh-coloured as in your or my flesh, not Brown's, as I don't think the headset manufacturers have started making them in fluorescent orange just yet.

As I said, when Allardyce wears his, the cameras spot other members of his staff in the stands with theirs on. I do believe he is actually using it. With other managers, I have never seen any of their coaches with a similar appliance sat in the stands. So who the hell are the managers talking to or listening to? They couldn't just be wearing them for effect, could they? The manager could just dispense with the headset and sit in the stand rather than be in the technical area with his headset on. But the spotlight isn't on you as much if you sit in the stand watching the match rather than gesticulating wildly outside the dugout while gabbling into a microphone. Gestures and a headset show to the fans that the manager is in charge. That he is the tactical genius behind the masterplan unfolding on the pitch in front of everybody. Either that, or it shows that he might be considering a job as a minicab controller for when he gets the sack after a brave but unsuccessful fight against relegation.

Some bosses use mobiles instead of headsets. They obviously have more credit than the headset wearers at the end of the week, and they also must have a very reliable network, because as anybody who has tried to do this knows, it is nigh on impossible even to send a text from a sporting occasion. Maybe all signals are blocked just to let the managers and coaching staff talk to one another in peace.

All this extra technological communication between the backroom staff makes them all look like spies in a Second World War film. As soon as they have to talk to each other their hands cover their mouths to avoid any of us mere mortals lip reading. The physio runs on to treat an injured player. He assesses the damage, then raises his talking device to his mouth. With his other hand, he covers his lips. Heaven forbid that any of us, fans, media, opposition, should realize that the player is going to have to go off with severe cramp. That has to remain top-secret, classified information.

The assistant manager is sat in the director's box. He phones down to the manager. The television cameras catch him doing this so he covers his mouth with his hand. We are assuming a vital tactical reorganization is required. It could equally be the number two passing on a message from the boss's wife about what he wants for tea when he gets home. That is so embarrassing that you can understand why he would be covering his mouth to pass that message on.

The result of introducing the technology is that the game suddenly appears more complex and more subtle. The message the headset-wearing, mobile-talking, hand-covering brigade are giving off is that hours of tactical planning have gone into each match. That they are aware and on their toes, ready to make even more changes as the game progresses. Not everybody can do this, they are saying, and certainly not you lot watching this match; only us very skilled, very technical people can manage this club. So don't criticize us, just watch and learn.

I don't think you would have caught Brian Clough wearing a headset. It wouldn't have complemented the green jersey for a start. But he also once said, 'Players lose you games, not tactics. There's so much crap talked about tactics by people who barely know how to win at dominoes.'

You may sympathize with his point or you may disagree, but he has missed out another factor that can lose you games. The man in the middle.

THE
AUTHORITIES

The Referee

I am assuming that you are reading this book sitting down. If, at this precise moment, you are stood up on public transport, trying to keep your balance while holding your bag and the book and desperately trying to avoid the sweaty armpit of the fat bloke stood next to you, then it might be best to stop reading now. What I am about to tell you could cause you to faint with shock, and I don't want that on my conscience. More importantly, I don't want a lawsuit against me because you fell over and hit your head on account of what you are about to read. *Where there's blame, there's a claim.*

Hopefully you are now sat down and comfortable and ready for the bombshell I am about to unleash.

Ready?

GRAHAM POLL IS A VERY NICE MAN

Deep breaths, everybody. Call somebody near by to fan you gently to get over the shock. Go and lie down in a darkened room for ten minutes before resuming this chapter, because you did read it correctly. Graham Poll is a very nice man. Yes, 'The Thing from Tring', 'The King of the Three Card Trick', 'Neil Warnock's Best Mate' can be most pleasant, and, worryingly, I now count him as a friend. The first time we met he gave me a signed copy of his auto-biography *Seeing Red*, which struck me as slightly egotistical, but apart from that I only have good things to say about him.

We met in the summer of 2008, ahead of the European Championship. The production company Bite Yer Legs had brought us together to present a twice-weekly podcast on the tournament taking place in Switzerland and Austria. The idea was for me to be irreverent and sarcastic, and to this end Graham was there for me to take the piss out of. And much as I did take the piss (his failure to send off a Croatian at the 2006 World Cup despite showing him two yellow cards cropped up a lot), Graham could give it as well as take it. He was also excellent at explaining refereeing decisions to me, why certain things were given and why others weren't. He was insightful, funny and good company.

If he is reading this then he will be a nightmare when I next see him, so, Graham, I'm afraid the compliments are going to have to stop here. Because all of this begs the question, if he is insightful, funny and good company, then why, when he was refereeing, was he such a nob at times? Why are they *all* such nobs at times?

It is difficult to know where to begin with referees. I do not want this to be one long rant (why change the habit of the book? you are probably saying), but I find that most of my problems with the men in black, yellow, green, blue, red or whatever shirt they are choosing to wear this season are encapsulated in one man. David Elleray.

I have never met Elleray, nor do I ever plan to, but I imagine that if I were to meet him, we would not instantly bond. I probably wouldn't consider him to be a very nice man and he would probably treat me like something he had just stepped in. This is all supposition of course, but he refereed in that way, as if he was superior to all others on the pitch. He is by no means alone among referees in carrying an air of superiority, but *his* air of superiority was superior to all other officials'.

Elleray refereed in the top flight of English football from 1986 to 2003, including an FA Cup Final in 1994, and in all that time I struggle to remember him smiling with a player or even engaging in a conversation. The refereeing fraternity would tell you that they aren't on a football field to smile or crack jokes, they are there to let the game flow and keep the players in check. But keeping them in check does not have to mean treating them like three-year-olds. Maybe instead of yellow cards there should be a naughty step they can put the players on for five minutes until they calm down and say sorry. Actually, they have that system in rugby, except they call it the sin bin.

Elleray combined his refereeing duties throughout the nineties with his other job, teaching. He wasn't a teacher at any ordinary school. He wasn't in charge of a South London comprehensive next to a sink estate where he had to confront the realities of everyday life. Oh no. He was a teacher at

Harrow School. One of the most privileged schools in the country. In fact, it is so posh that he isn't actually referred to as a teacher but a schoolmaster. I have no interest in discussing the differences between the public and private education systems, that is far too serious and highbrow for a throwaway book like this, but I do think they influenced the way Mr Elleray – or should that be Sir Elleray – took charge of games.

It was as if he expected 'yes sir' and 'no sir' from the players, in the same manner as his pupils probably addressed him. There was to be no answering back, no room for discussion, and his decision was final. As a fan watching on, it looked like the players were not allowed to question anything. If they did, they were booked. It was as if Robbie Savage, Vinnie Jones, Roy Keane et al. were pupils at his school, although you couldn't envisage them with straw boaters on their heads skipping over the hill to their next lesson. (Thinking about it, I could see Savage doing that.) Elleray would argue that his style of refereeing allowed him to keep control of the game and that the players always knew who was in charge. Roy Keane certainly knew who was in charge because Elleray sent him off four times in his career.

My problem with this style of officiating is that it immediately creates a them-and-him situation. The players' hackles are raised because they know that the referee is going to treat them like small children and they won't be able to talk to him. By this I don't mean being able to argue with the referee, just to talk to him and ask, 'Why have you given that, ref?' or 'Why haven't you played on there, ref?' or 'I didn't touch him, ref.' (These sentences might have come from *The Famous Five Play Football* they sound so twee, but I didn't want to use gratuitous swearing.) The schoolmasterly style of refereeing hasn't disappeared with Elleray's retirement. There are still those who follow his lead, and they are the ones the fans dread taking charge of their team's games.

Is the schoolmasterly approach worse than the referee who thinks he is *the* man, that all eyes are going to be on him, that he is the person who could make or break the game of football he is about to take charge of? I was playing for my amateur side last season. We were coming to the end of the campaign, there was nothing on the game because we had already been relegated, the sun was shining and we were looking forward to a good game of football and enjoying ourselves before a summer of having to spend Saturdays with our families rather than our team-mates. As I stood by the centre circle, waiting for kick-off, I turned to the referee and said, 'Have a good game, ref.'

'I always do,' came the reply. No smile, no irony, just deadly serious arrogance.

'Nob,' I thought, and nob he was. The next ninety minutes was all about him rather than the game. Whereas I try to base my game on a mixture of Eric Cantona and Mark Hughes, he was obviously basing his game on a mixture of Jeff Winter and Uriah Rennie. He was more successful.

You don't think of amateur referees having heroes just like fans or amateur players. I don't think anything of team-mates wearing certain boots because they are the same as Ronaldo's or Titus Bramble's. I don't think anything of grown men going to games in replica shirts with the name and number of their favourite player on. But a referee showing hero worship is, quite frankly, ridiculous.

As any amateur footballer will tell you, at our level there are three types of referee: the acne-ridden fourteen-year-olds who are just starting out and probably aren't good enough to play; the massively unfit lumps who are too fat to play; and finally the ones you fear might die out on the pitch with you as they are pushing ninety and any movement outside the centre circle leaves them gasping for breath for the next half hour.

On the occasion of watching our fourth team away a few years ago, the referee fell very firmly, snugly even, into the middle category. The fourth team were grateful even to have a referee because normally the substitute or the manager has to take charge of the first half with his opposite number doing the second. The fourth team is all about having fun; the social side is more important than the actual game. It will come as no surprise, then, that the team actually met the referee in the bar before the match. He wasn't drinking, but I can't say the same for some of our players. Forget Lucozade, Powerade, Gatorade, BandAid and the rest, Fosters is the fuel of choice for the fourth team. The referee was genial enough and big enough. If Peter Kay hadn't been flogging his arse around the country trying to buy his mum a bungalow at the time I would have sworn it was him refereeing that day at Kew Gardens. (It is a posh league.)

With our team warming up – a few stretches, a few passing drills, then twenty minutes trying to get our one and only ball out of a hedge after our centre-half had tried to control it – we awaited the arrival of the official. At this level, they normally come out in some ill-fitting kit. On this occasion I was expecting it to be particularly ill fitting. It wasn't, though. Peter trotted on to the pitch in a resplendent replica kit from the 2002 World Cup in Japan and South Korea. Complete with all the appropriate badges.

I had never realized replica referee kits from the major tournaments were sold. I'd also never realized that you could get referee kits in such large sizes. Then I remembered that Graham had refereed at that tournament. Graham might have been his refereeing hero, or he might have just wanted a nice kit. Either way he was leaving himself open to an awful lot of piss-taking by walking on to a dog-turd-covered pitch for a game of football between two fourth teams, a few of whom had had a beer, dressed as a World Cup referee.

He didn't do too badly during the course of the game. He wasn't at World Cup standard, but then neither was Graham at the actual World Cup. He did a decent job, and he did this decent job without what appears to be the most important aide to a referee in the modern game. No, I am not talking about linesmen – sorry, assistant referees, but something that our Premier League referees now cannot do without or be seen without. Our old friend the headset.

Over the past few years we have been treated to sweaty middle-aged men running around our Premier League pitches looking like they are going to start Vogue-ing. They should complete the Madonna look they are going for by wearing conical bras. The headsets involve one large earpiece and then a thin strip of a microphone that is connected via a wire to the earpiece and sits just below the chin or chins of the person wearing it. They come in two colours, black or a pink/peachy colour.

The thinking behind this highly technical piece of equipment – and it is highly technical, despite my rather poor description making it sound like a child's toy from Argos – is that it should improve communication between the officials. To that end, the referee's microphone is constantly on and the assistants and 4th official have a button they push if they want to talk. The reason? They don't want any noise coming from the technical area, where the 4th official stands, to distract the referee from his decision-making.

All sounds good, doesn't it? It sounds like a decent system that should work well. Except, have you ever seen them use the blooming things? I am sure they have in the odd match, it's just I can't recall ever having seen it. Whenever I see a referee needing to consult with one of his linesmen, he runs over to talk to him. Why? You are all wearing a hi-tech communication system. Save your legs and get your lino, in the words of the Sugababes, to push the button.

The problem with the system is that it is for show. The powers-that-be seem to be under the impression that sticking an earpiece and a microphone on a referee makes them seem more official, more responsible and more in touch with our ultra-modern, fast-paced society. In fact it makes them look like a cross between a call centre worker and David Coleman's *Spitting Image* puppet. (For the benefit of younger readers, Coleman was a legendary BBC commentator whose puppet permanently had its finger pushing an earpiece into its ear.)

Running over to talk to the linesman or 4th official is for show as well, though. The referee needs to be seen to be using his team to help him with controversial decisions. He needs to be seen to be a team player and a dictator, like a refereeing equivalent of Mussolini. He could talk to his team over the headsets but then the people in the ground wouldn't see that, so he has to make a point of running over to one of his team for a discussion, rendering the headset obsolete. QED – they are pointless.

The 4th Official

But not as pointless as the 4th official. I have no idea what the job description of the 4th official is in the *Referee's Handbook* but I would imagine it's something like 'Spend the full ninety minutes of the game getting on everybody's tits'. If the referee can be annoying and officious during a game then you can multiply that tenfold for the 4th official.

I have done some research for this section, and I can tell you the role of the 4th official came into being in 1995. It was introduced one year after some bright spark at FIFA devised the technical area. Dugouts were getting bigger and substitutes more numerous and somebody needed to control it all. The 4th official is basically a glorified traffic warden. He is there to make sure that nobody, bar the subs who want to warm up, moves out of the marked box in front of the dugouts. As soon as a manager or assistant manager is up off the bench to bark orders at the players then the 4th official is up as well, at his side, to make sure he doesn't step over the white lines of the area. Are there not more important things for them to worry about? Could they not help the referee on the pitch by being an extra pair of eyes? Would it not be better for them to watch the game for something the referee has missed, rather than policing a small box that is off the pitch? It can't help the manager either. There he is, trying to explain to a midfielder that he wants him to push further forward, when he is rudely interrupted by somebody telling him his left foot has gone six inches over the line and could he take a step back.

But is the 4th official who is strict and pedantic better than the 4th official who tries to ingratiate himself with the benches and get involved in some matey banter? Shortly after Alan Shearer took over at Newcastle to try to save them from Premier League relegation, the club had a home game, and according to my friend sat behind the St James's Park dugout, the 4th official tried to stick as close as possible to Shearer. He laughed and joked his way through the ninety minutes as he attempted to become Shearer's best mate. Just what the former England captain needed. He was new to management, desperately trying to keep his hometown club up, and he had somebody with him thinking it was one big laugh. Shearer was criticized for his language after that game, and he apologized for it. Given what he'd had to put up with, no apology was needed.

There could be a perfect role for the 4th official so that he isn't deemed officious or an annoying joker, and you only have to look to cricket for the way he can be used. The 3rd umpire looks at TV evidence. He helps the two on-field umpires on controversial decisions such as run-outs and stumpings. His role has enhanced the game no end.

Thanks to Sepp Blatter, this won't be the case in football.

In June 2009, Blatter decreed that the 4th official would no longer have a monitor. He would therefore be denied the chance to see replays of any controversial incidents that occurred on the pitch. Blatter took his decision after a Confederations Cup match between Egypt and Brazil. It was refereed by Howard Webb. Webb is a policeman and easily the best ref in England. He is authoritative, intelligent and an engaging official. He is strict, fair and uses his common sense. Towards the end of this game, Webb signalled for a corner to Brazil. He then changed his mind after being told that an Egyptian player had handled on the line and gave a penalty. It was scored, and Brazil won 4–3. The Egyptian officials subsequently complained that Webb had changed his mind on the advice of the 4th official, who had seen a replay. In fact, Webb had been given a signal by his assistant referee that the handball had occurred (I am not sure whether this was done over the headset or face to face). Blatter didn't like the insinuation that it had come from the 4th official and decided that to avoid confusion in the future he would make sure monitors weren't in the eyeline of the man patrolling the technical area.

This incident followed on from the World Cup Final three years earlier when it was widely reported, although always denied, that the 4th official had contributed to the sending off of Zinedine Zidane. It looked like the referee had missed Zidane's headbutt on the Italian centre-half Marco Materazzi and that it was only once the 4th official had seen a television replay that the man in the middle took action.

Whether the 4th official was involved in either of these decisions is irrelevant. The point is that on both occasions the referee took the right decision. The use of technology in football is a very old and very dull argument. I advocate its use not for the good of the game but for the good of the 4th official and the sanity of the managers. Put a monitor in front of the 4th official and tell him to look out for anything controversial or anything that might help the man in the middle. That would allow managers to pass on instructions without worrying about the position of their feet, and it would allow Alan Shearer to manage without suffering a stream of knock-knock gags.

Of course, the 4th official would have to leave his position next to a monitor to perform his other massively important job: working the electronic board. This is quite possibly the most pointless piece of technology introduced to the game. We can't have goal-line cameras but we can have green and red flashing numbers on an LED display. Brilliant!

This board has two functions: to inform the crowd about substitutions, and to tell them how much stoppage time is to be played at the end of each half.

Pre-Premier League and pre-squad numbers, no such thing was needed for substitutions. Some bloke, normally associated with the team making the change, would hold up a massive piece of card with the number of the player coming off, and that would be that. No need to put up the number of the player coming on because he was always wearing number 12. Now, with squad numbers and multiple substitutions, this is no longer possible. Up to six times per game we are confronted with the sight of a man resembling your dad trying to work out how the TV remote functions. After several years of working with these boards you would have thought they would know how to work them, but oh no. You still see the 4th official delaying substitutions as he works out how to programme his board and tries to remember whether the number that is coloured red is the player coming on or going off. Once programmed and the substitution is ready to go ahead, there is something that the 4th official seems to have perfected: no matter who is doing it, he always manages to hold the board at such an angle that you can't actually see the numbers and can't make out who is coming on and who is coming off.

And you don't even have to be looking at the boards to find out the amount of stoppage time at the end of each half. It will always be one minute added on at the end of the first period and four minutes at the end of the second. The only exception – and you would be disappointed if I didn't put this easy joke in – is at Old Trafford, where United will get at least six minutes at the end of the second half if they aren't winning.

A referee is meant to include stoppages for injuries and to add on thirty seconds for each substitution. Then, with a couple of minutes to go at the end of each half, he signals to the 4th official how much time he is going to add on. Surely it would be easier to tell him over the headset rather than subtly placing fingers across his thigh or his arm as if he was giving the number of syllables in a game of charades. I reckon most of the time the 4th official isn't looking at his mate in the middle and just thinks 'Sod it, it's the first half, I'll add on a minute' or 'Sod it, it's the second half, I'll give it an extra four.'

It might not be exactly like this, but we don't know, do we, because the men, and women, involved in officiating are not allowed to talk to the media. We can't find out their thoughts, their reasoning behind their decisions or even the rules they are applying because they have to keep quiet. Frighteningly, working with Graham Poll for a couple of years has been an education. It has allowed me to see what goes on in the minds of our officials (not a lot, obviously) and how they have to work within the rules – not just the rules of the game but the rules on how they must officiate.

I filmed a video for the FA in 2008 to promote their Respect campaign. All the big names in showbiz were involved, Mark Durden-Smith, Ben Shepherd and Steve Claridge to name just three. The aforementioned Howard Webb was there as well. I spent a lot of time talking to him and we exchanged numbers and are now text buddies. (Again, please don't think I am name dropping here.) Even with the odd text I understand better how he has refereed a game and why he has made certain decisions. Why can't he make his thoughts known to the outside world? The body who looks after our officials wants them to remain silent. They cannot see the advantages of a referee talking to the media.

Most of us do not know all the rules. We think we know all the rules but we don't. Interviews with referees would help improve that knowledge. More importantly, though, we would see them as human beings. Howard has a broad Yorkshire accent and a surprisingly deep voice. You probably didn't know that. He also has a dry sense of humour. You definitely didn't know that. As soon as we start hearing from them we start to see them less as schoolmasterly, arrogant idiots and more as men trying their best to do a very difficult job. Most of them aren't dictators, they aren't power-mad egotists, and at the same time they are not Trappist monks. Let them talk. Although not David Elleray, because nothing could improve my perception of him, nor of all the referees who have sent me off in my amateur career. They were all nobs.

Sepp Blatter

I hope that so far I have not singled anybody out for too much criticism. Except David Elleray. Not one section has been directed at purely one man. The game as it was and the game as it is are our collective responsibilities. Until now. Now is the time to unleash my wrath on one man.

I feel I will struggle to get much warmth into this because the man in question is not a loveable rogue with faults like the rest of us. This is a man who every time he opens his mouth comes across as a complete and utter – well, you know by now the noun I would use to describe him. And worryingly, this is not a man who has some minor role in the sport. Oh no. This man is in charge of the global game. The big boss. This man is the President of FIFA.

Joseph S. Blatter, born in Switzerland in 1936, is not any old man. He is a cross between Bill Gates, Kofi Annan and Princess Diana . . . if you believe his profile on the FIFA website. Now, obviously you wouldn't expect the organization's official website to be critical of its own president, but it does portray him as a modern-day saint living within our midst.

We should be lucky to have him on this planet, let alone to have him leading our sport. Except we shouldn't because under Blatter's reign the game has become a plaything for the rich and powerful. The gap between the big and the small continues to grow ever wider and the sport is step by step moving away from the fans and players and into the hands of the authorities. I fear he won't stop until he is omnipotent.

To succeed in the sporting world, you need an ego. To become a top-class player, you need to believe that you are a top-class player. To become a top-class manager, you need to believe you have the skills to make people want to play for you. To write a book full of sporting ramblings and moans, you have to believe that people actually want to read the guff you are writing. To become the FIFA President, you have to believe that you are the most important man in the game.

The FIFA website is very keen to explain to us the amazing education the multilingual Blatter received. He gained a degree in Business Administration and Economics from the Faculty of Law at Lausanne University. It is written as something to be proud of, whereas to me it sounds like hell on earth as it includes administration, economics and law all in the same sentence. It doesn't scream out that this man has a feel for football. It screams out that he is not somebody you would want to get stuck next to sat on the bus. Not that Blatter gets the bus, of course. Expenses, limousines and turning left rather than right on aircraft are all part and parcel of the FIFA gravy train – that's if planes and cars can be part of a train when the previous sentence began by talking about buses.

There have been allegations of corruption and financial mismanagement, and if you are hoping now for a thorough investigation into those claims then you really should know me better than that by now and you have bought the wrong book. I am steering well clear of those kind of allegations, because firstly I am a fan and the financial management of football doesn't massively interest fans and is best left to journalists on broadsheet newspapers, and secondly, when a book is published that goes into the subject of Blatter, FIFA can try to stop it being published.

In 2006, after four years of research (four years! I have found four days perfectly adequate), Andrew Jennings wrote *Foul! The Secret World of FIFA: Bribes, Vote Rigging and Ticket Scandals*. Something, and it is difficult to gauge what it was exactly, gave FIFA an inkling that the book wasn't going to be complimentary about them or the Blatter regime so they took out an injunction to stop it being published. Only in Switzerland. I can only assume they chose to ban it in Switzerland because FIFA is based in Zurich and not because they felt that skiers who read the book over their lunchtime rösti and glühwein wouldn't be able to concentrate on the slopes in the afternoon because of thoughts of financial mis-management. As it is, I know of three people in Switzerland – Davos, to be exact – who would love to read this book and therefore I don't want to risk a ban in Europe's favourite neutral country by investigating FIFA's books.

There is nothing contentious about suggesting Blatter's love of a committee. If there is a problem in the game, then set up a committee to investigate. To this end, he is no different to any town council in the land. But Blatter is in charge of the greatest game in the world, not my rubbish collection. Football is fast, immediate and fun and is increasingly being bogged down in bureaucracy. When there was a call in 2002 to investigate FIFA's finances, Blatter set up a committee. He subsequently suspended that committee around the time he was up for re-election. He took the decision to disband it. We should be grateful for that, and that he didn't set up a committee to see whether the original committee needed to be stopped.

FIFA's website actually considers the use of committees to be a good thing. 'FIFA's General Secretary is assisted in his or her work by more than 25 standing committees', it states, 'and by two judicial bodies, the FIFA Disciplinary Committee and the FIFA Appeal Committee.' 'The committees serve a crucial function,' it continues, 'to generally take all the fun out of the game, bugger up your enjoyment of it and leave us all weighed down by red tape.' (I have added that last bit.) Is it any wonder we now have a sport so full of inconsistencies across the globe, a sport where the rich get richer, where children are poached from one country to another, where more and more tournaments are introduced for the sake of money? A simple game cannot be kept simple when its world governing body needs twenty-five committees to run it.

Imagine the chaos the game could dissolve into if FIFA no longer had the Futsal and Beach Soccer Committee. That committee should also have a word with itself for calling it soccer and not football. I personally would see a grave future for the sport if FIFA got rid of its Goal Development Officers. The Emergency Commitee must be permanently rushed off its feet, though I do imagine them to be sat there like firemen enjoying tea and biscuits and all sleeping in bunk beds waiting for the 999 call. Meanwhile, the Ethics Committee are obviously doing their jobs very well because the game is ethically sound, isn't it? Although if the Ethics Committee are snowed under and need to ease their workload then they could call on the Committee for Fair Play and Social Responsibility. They probably do exactly the same thing while at the same time allowing more people to make money out of football while doing absolutely bugger all good.

Those are all at a world level. If we drop down to European level and look at UEFA then things are slightly better. They only have fifteen committees listed on their website, including the delightfully named Meridian Project Board, which I can only assume is dedicated to improving ITV coverage on the south coast, an honourable mission if ever there was one. Oh, but wait. There are only fifteen committees because they also use panels. They have twenty-two panels at the last count including (and there are a few good ones coming up here) the Refereeing Certification Panel – yes, it takes a whole room of grown men to issue a certificate, and I would imagine a badge for the referee to sew on his trunks; the Football Turf Experts Panel – men locked in a room choosing which is the best grass (who knew UEFA had so much in common with many a South London estate?); and the best one, the Administrative

Experts Panel. I am assured it is a laugh a minute with those guys.

I cannot hold Sepp Blatter responsible for all of this. Michel Platini is Blatter's equivalent at UEFA and should shoulder some of the blame. Yet, I like Platini. He is portrayed in the media in this country as anti-English. The main reason I can see for this conclusion is that he is French. I don't believe it. His aim – an honourable one, however futile it may seem – is to try and make football a level playing field, not a sport that is dominated by the rich and the powerful. He doesn't want clubs in debt, he doesn't want children poached from country to country, and he doesn't want the champions of Albania to miss out on top European competition because they are based in Albania and not finishing fourth in Germany. It is a refreshing view from somebody so powerful. He was also one of the best players the world has ever seen and I have affection for him because I remember him playing and remember him in action in my favourite World Cup of all time, España 82. I can't say the same about Blatter.

My final reason for admiring Platini while despairing of the little Swiss fella is that the Frenchman doesn't talk crap every time he opens his mouth. Blatter most definitely does. He suffers from an affliction that can affect a lot of people in power. It is commonly known as foot in mouth disease but can also be a desperate attempt to please whichever audience he is addressing at the time. So, he has suggested to the Americans splitting the game into four quarters instead of two halves; he has suggested making the goals bigger; and he has told one country how good a host of the World Cup they would be before then travelling days later to another country in the running and telling them how good a host they would be. It is as if he isn't aware that his comments will be repeated around the globe no matter where he has made them. But that is what tends to happen when you are the leader of world football.

There are two comments he has made that will always be mentioned when he is spoken about. The first came in the summer of 2008 when Cristiano Ronaldo was angling for a move from Manchester United to Real Madrid. Alex Ferguson was adamant they were not going to sell him. The player was staying at Old Trafford. In waded Blatter, to liken Ronaldo's situation to modern-day slavery. In one fell swoop he managed to offend the majority of the footballing community. Manchester United were furious at his intervention, and the racial connotations that come with the word 'slavery' caused offence among black players past and present. Pelé joined the debate, saying, 'You are a slave if you work without a contract or you don't get paid.' Fans were reading Blatter's comments on one page of their newspaper, then turning the page to see photos of the enslaved Ronaldo sunning his perfect six-pack on a lounger while surrounded by various women wearing dental floss to cover their most delicate places. The only person who came out in agreement with Blatter was . . . Ronaldo. What a surprise.

Blatter most likely approved of the attire of Ronaldo's female companions in the sun because his most famous inappropriate comment involved women. And women footballers in particular. In 2004, the head of FIFA, whose organization has a Women's Football Committee (I know that will come as a shock), issued his plan to improve the women's game. It didn't involve more funding, greater grass-roots involvement or the improvement of the structure of competitions across the world. It involved instead hotpants. He wanted the women to wear tighter shorts to 'promote a more female aesthetic'. He wanted them to use beach volley-ball as an example. Among the brickbats hurled back at him was 'typical bloke', which is offensive to all us typical blokes. What it was was a typical comment from a man who in the 1970s was President of the World Society of the Friends of Suspenders. This was an organization set up in protest against the rise of women wearing tights in preference to stockings and suspenders. The man who now runs world football was once a man who really cared about what women wear under their skirts. Need I say anything else on the Blatter?

The Premier League

Jimmy was several years above me at school. He was a foot-baller, a football fan, and somebody who took me under his wing. I thought he was cool, he more than likely thought I wasn't. Yet he was always great with me. He once took me to Old Trafford and we stood. It was electrifying and exciting. It felt new and dangerous and I felt like a real grown-up. Then, I felt wet. My feet felt really really sodden. Rather than go to the loo, somebody a few levels back had unleashed himself, and I was stood in the result. It wasn't as bad as a few years later when somebody at an REM gig in Huddersfield pissed in my pocket, but that's a story for another book. So whenever the Premier League is cast as the mother of all evils, the symbol of everything that is wrong in the modern game, I have to disagree. I have never ever ended up stood in a puddle of someone else's urine at a Premier League game, and that can only be a good thing.

The critics state that the competition is becoming boring because only a handful of clubs have won the title. Four, in fact, since it started: Manchester United, Blackburn Rovers,

Arsenal and Chelsea. At the time of writing, that's four winners in the seventeen years the competition has been going. In the final seventeen years of the First Division there were six different winners: Liverpool, Arsenal, Nottingham Forest, Everton, Aston Villa and Leeds United. There isn't that much difference.

Oh, but clubs came from nowhere to win the league when it was the First Division, the critics say, nobody could do a Nottingham Forest now. Nobody could come up from a division below from a smallish place in England and take the title. Blackburn Rovers did. Chelsea hadn't won the title for fifty years when they got their hands on it. Just because they are now considered to be one of the heavyweights of the game doesn't mean they have always been that way. Manchester City look set to be one of the game's big guns in the coming years. They haven't exactly been dripping in success over the years. As the Inspiral Carpets-inspired United chant goes, 'This is how it feels to be City. This is how it feels to be small. This is how it feels when your team wins nothing at all.'

The other main criticism is that the Premier League has now created a massive gap between themselves and the rest of the footballing community. There was always that gap. If you are running four divisions then it stands to reason that the top division will be better off and of better quality than the others. It isn't called a competition for nothing. There has to be the strong and the weak. Even in the carefully structured NFL, with its 'everybody is equal' mentality, there are teams that have been crap for years. Yes, there are different winners, and yes, the big teams go through spells of struggling and not winning, but for the San Francisco 49ers, you could read Liverpool. Both are trying to re-create the glory days of the 1980s.

And the gap between the haves and have-nots could actually be worse. The Premier League, to their credit, implements a twenty-club television deal. The rights are negotiated as a collective. Half the money is split equally between the twenty of them, another quarter goes on prize money, and the final quarter is paid per television appearance. Overseas rights are split equally. It does mean that the bigger clubs, or the more successful clubs, earn more, but the system is a lot fairer than the ones operated in Spain and Italy where clubs can negotiate their own television deals. In that structure, the big get bigger and the small get smaller. Real Madrid can command a lot more money for their TV rights than Real Valladolid. Similarly, AC Milan tend to get more euros coming into the coffers than Livorno.

The men who run the Premier League will argue that they do everything possible to increase opportunities, to promote their product and to maximize revenue streams. Indeed, part of their mission statement goes as follows: 'The Premier League must generate increased commercial value, using the resulting revenues to further enhance our competitions and strengthen the long-term future of the Premier League and its clubs.'

And at this point I can't defend it any longer. There is no mention of football there. It has ceased to be a sport in some eyes and is now a product or a business where we are no longer fans but consumers. Money is the be-all and end-all. How can we make more? Where can we make more? From whom can we make more? We, as fans, are expected to go along with it because, after all, what do we know? We are there to be patronized and patted on the head like three-year-olds, told to run along and enjoy the game but leave the running and the organizing to the men who know what they are doing. The game is taken ever further from us and we can't come close to grabbing some of it back because we are kept at a distance by the game's powerbrokers.

I say the game is taken ever further away, it nearly went to the other side of the world to get away from us. In 2008, the chief executive of the Premier League, Richard Scudamore, suggested a thirty-ninth game in the season. It would involve all the clubs playing one extra game in another part of the world. So, you could have Everton against Liverpool in Bangkok, or Spurs against Chelsea in Dubai. If you were really lucky and lived in Melbourne you might get Bolton against Stoke. Logistically it would be a nightmare, it would make the competition unbalanced and unfair, and in the example above it could set back Anglo-Australian relations years.

I have only met Scudamore once and found him to be an interesting bloke to talk to. He is a man who has his twenty member clubs' best interests at heart, and by that I mean he wants to make as much money for them as possible. I am all for sports trying to innovate. I adore rugby league, and that sport has been the most innovative of all over the past twenty years. From substitutions to sin bins, video replays to an independent timekeeper, league did it first. However, when league innovates, it never forgets its roots. Scudamore's plan was doing just that.

Come up with ideas, put them out there, encourage debate, but never ever forget the roots of the game and the roots of the clubs you are trying to send out to Hong Kong or Tokyo. I featured Manchester City chief executive Gary Cook's comments earlier in the book. Scudamore's plan provoked a similar reaction in me.

I support my club because I am from that area. A Bolton fan tends to support Bolton because he is from Bolton. There certainly aren't many cockney glory-hunting Wanderers fans. They go week in, week out to watch their team, to support their team, and to reveal proudly to the world that they are from Bolton. This is their club, their area. This is who they are. What right has somebody in Detroit to watch a game live involving their club? Do they understand the history? Do they understand the area? Do they understand the passion? I would venture the answer to all of those questions is no.

I don't give a shit that somebody in Beijing has bought a Manchester United shirt and that that has put forty quid into the club's accounts. I don't give a shit that somebody in the UAE has bought a subscription to MUTV. Good for them. If they want Terry Christian in their lounge then who am I to argue? But it does not mean that my club should go out there to reward them. I don't get rewards for supporting my club. I actually have to pay a lot of bloody money to support my club and don't get any thanks for it, and I don't want any. I just want to be able to watch them home and away in my own country.

I have a horrible feeling that that comes across as xenophobic and right-wing. It isn't meant to. Even in a multi-billion-pound sport, football clubs should be part of the community. They should be a force for good. They know that, though, and the Premier League knows that too, which is why so many of them are involved in charity projects and why the Premier League funds so many projects to help the disadvantaged. You have to dig around to find out about those projects though, which is probably as much a fault of the media as it is the authorities. We don't like reporting good news as much as bad!

It is said a nation gets the politicians it deserves, which means we have been a very bad country, but does the football community get the rulers it deserves? From a club point of view, it does. Money is the be-all and end-all of the game. The fans, though, do not get the rulers they deserve. The Premier League could do with relaxing a little bit, realizing that football is meant to be fun, that it should be a sport first and a business second. All we ask for is a bit of respect. Don't treat us like idiots in a smug manner, we know a thing or two about this game as well. Just because you have run GlaxoSmithKline doesn't mean you can run football. Don't take our clubs, our teams, around the world chasing the dollar. It is already a multi-billion-pound industry, how much more money do you need or want?

Smile, enjoy the game and watch the football on offer rather than thinking about the next deal you can make, that would be my advice to our leaders. And to you, dear reader, next time you slag off Richard Scudamore, which you will – we all will – look on the bright side and be grateful he was never part of a campaign group to do with women's underwear.

Tournament Draws

I feel we got a bit deep in the last little section. It was a bit heavy and a bit of a rant, so let's change mood by talking balls. Lots of balls.

I don't remember how draws for tournaments were done when I was a kid. I certainly never watched one of them. England just magically appeared in a World Cup group with France, Kuwait and Czechoslovakia, or in a European qualifying group with Denmark and Hungary. Manchester United always came out in the FA Cup against Bournemouth, and I just accepted it. I think I may have listened to the FA Cup draw on Radio Two, but we weren't a Radio Two family. I assume all of these draws took place in little back rooms, undertaken by old men in blazers and one man with a clipboard. The clipboard remains, but there is much more of a song and dance to these things now. They are proper events. Sometimes they are actually more entertaining than the tournament itself.

There are four types of draw. There are the draws for the international tournaments like the World Cup and European

Championship, then you have the draw for the European club competitions, followed by the draw for domestic cup competitions, and finally the draw for the Johnstone's Paint Trophy.

The Johnstone's Paint Trophy is approximately the seventeenth different name for the competition in its short history. It is a cup fought over only by the sides in the bottom two divisions and for that reason isn't taken too seriously. At least I am assuming it isn't taken too seriously because the draw for the tournament resembles *Play Your Cards Right*. Without Bruce Forsyth. And without the Dolly Dealers. And without a chance to go for the car for that matter. But it still rips off *Play Your Cards Right*. Each club's badge is printed on to a giant playing card. They are then shuffled, put on a rack and drawn by the presenters of *Soccer AM*, who take on the Dolly Dealer roles for the purpose of this event.

Out of all the draws, the one for this tournament is the one most likely to go wrong. In previous draws, the set has fallen down and caused chaos with cards tumbling everywhere, and before it took place on *Soccer AM* it was handled by Radio Five Live. One year at the semi-final stage, a team was drawn to play itself after the newsreader put the ball back in the bag after the first time she'd picked it out. That is probably why all other draws are left to the professionals. Or should I say ex-professionals.

When the FA Cup draw was first televised it was presided over by a man called Graham Kelly. If you don't know who Graham Kelly is then think of the least likely person you know who could present on television. Imagine somebody with no bounce, no enthusiasm and a droning voice who looks like he works in IT and spends most of his days working on hard drives in a basement. Then multiply all of that by ten and you are close to getting the presenting style of Graham Kelly. He was also chief executive of the FA, by the way. It was easily the most painful ten minutes of television of the week. If there was a saving grace with Kelly it was that he didn't try and build his part up. He was there to drone that 'number twenty-three, Sheffield United' would play 'number forty-seven, Luton Town'.

When Kelly eventually left, to continue his career on the after-dinner circuit, he was replaced as Master of Ceremonies by David Davies. Davies was a dangerous combination of TV presenter and journalist turned football administrator. He had the authority to conduct the draw with the ego of somebody who was on the box. He resembled the father of the bride on the microphone at a wedding. This was his moment, and he was going to make the most of it and crack some funnies. He couldn't just say 'number twelve, Portsmouth'. Oh no. For him it had to be 'number twelve, Portsmouth, on the south coast there'. No shit, Sherlock. Portsmouth is on the south coast, is it? All I care about is who they are going to play, not their geographical location. Unfortunately, this 'hilarity' would spread across the room and the ex-professionals would feel obliged to join in and add their own witticisms. These continue to this day, and I guarantee that neither a Carling Cup draw nor an FA Cup draw will pass by without all of the following happening.

The first ex-pro involved will be drawing the home teams. He will also be in charge of tipping the balls out of the velvet bag into a giant Perspex bowl that looks like part of the game Kerplunk. And here comes the first gag. The second ex-pro or the presenter, who is no longer David Davies, will suggest that one ball has been left in the bag. Cue a quick fiddle in the bag just to check, and mirth all round.

Then the draw begins. What we are looking out for now is when the ex-pros draw the two clubs they are most associated with, because that is going to be hilarious. The first ex-pro might draw 'his' team at home. 'Oh, they'll be happy with you there,' says the presenter as the first ex-pro looks smug and the second ex-pro giggles. A few minutes later the second guy draws 'his' team away from home. 'Oh, they aren't going to be happy with you there,' says the presenter as the second ex-pro looks sheepish and the first ex-pro giggles. Of course there are variations on this theme. Sometimes the ex-professionals draw each other's team which can be very funny too. But the maximum hilarity, the Del-Boy-falling-through-the-bar moment, is when the two ex-professionals draw their teams to play each other. When that happens, sides are in danger of splitting up and down the country. And on top of all this, the host is still providing those valuable snippets of information. 'Number thirteen, Newcastle, up there in the north-east' will play 'number twenty-four, Port Vale, who are, erm . . . who are, erm, erm . . . of course near Stoke'.

For a while they flirted with a live studio audience watch-ing the draw as it happened, but when television executives realized they weren't enjoying themselves quite as much as the three people involved and would rather be sat in a pub having their Sunday lunch, they quickly disbanded the idea. Now they just rely on sticking cameras at the smaller clubs still left in the draw, hoping to get scenes of rapturous joy and grown men hugging one another as the non-league heroes get drawn away to Liverpool. More often than not, though, you are left with a group of men sat in a club board-room, with a lovely buffet laid out behind them, trying to look excited at having drawn Scunthorpe away.

There is very little you can do to make pulling balls out of a box exciting – ask any cricketer – so although we can take the mickey a lot, we can't really criticize. And we should be grateful that the draws for our domestic cup competitions are mercifully short and simple. When you go up a level to European competition, you need a degree in advanced mathematics and the patience of a saint.

You would have thought that putting thirty-two teams from across Europe into the eight Champions League groups for that stage of the competition would be quite simple. Pick them out, pop them into a group, and go home. Thank you very much. Not with UEFA.

Of course, there is a committee that puts all this together. It is the Club Competitions Committee. They met several years ago when the group stage was increased to include thirty-two teams and came up with a few rules designed both to confuse and make sure the draw lasted as long as possible. So for this draw teams are seeded; teams from the same country are not allowed to be in the same group; for television purposes half the groups will play on a Tuesday night, the others on a Wednesday; only two teams per country can play on any given night; teams in red can't play teams in blue; teams with an average height of 5'10" can only be in groups A, B, C and D; Manchester United must always get the easiest group draw possible; and so it goes on. Rule after rule, meaning that when the draw takes place there are more balls flying about than at a swingers party.

Knowing that the draw is complicated and will take some time to execute, it would make sense to make everything surrounding the event as simple as possible. That isn't UEFA's way, and that isn't football's way. It becomes a show that makes you long for Graham Kelly or David Davies, as they unleash not one, not two, but three presenters on us. Well, two presenters and a model. Well, actually, one presenter, a model and an old bloke from UEFA.

The presenter over recent years has been a bloke off CNN, that well-respected football channel. CNN fulfils every stereotype on how Americans report on soccer, but UEFA employs one of their presenters, Pedro Pinto, on the basis that he looks good, sounds European, and pronounces everything in a really annoying way.

'But why would you need three presenters [well, one presenter, a model and an old bloke from UEFA] to host a football tournament draw?' I hear you ask. Well, my friend, this is because it is not just a draw but an awards ceremony as well. For reasons best known to nobody, the football glitterati are sat in a lecture hall in Monaco to pay homage to the goalkeeper, defender, midfielder and striker of the year.

It's not really of the year, as such, it is of the last Champions League campaign. Who on earth is going to win these prestigious titles nobody knows who has voted for, or indeed cares? My money is always on the goalkeeper, defender, midfielder and striker who are the only players sat there in the front row of the lecture hall.

Not only do they win their award, but each one of them has to participate in the draw, and that explains why they look so scared as they walk on to the stage. They are smiling, but in their heads they are thinking, 'If I had wanted to go on *The Krypton Factor* I would have written to Gordon Burns.' They are thrown helplessly and with no training into the hands of the UEFA old bloke and a world of balls and pots and letters and colours. It is daunting.

The draw begins. The men involved wish that UEFA could have designed better balls because they seem like a bugger to open. The goalkeeper of the year ends up looking like a man desperately trying to get his toy out of the yellow capsule inside a Kinder egg. It starts simply enough. It is only once the opening seeds have been drawn out that the fun and games begin.

Before each group of seeds is drawn out, Pedro nips back in and announces the winner of the next award. So the defender of the year will draw out the group of second seeds, the midfielder of the year the group of third seeds, and the glory award, the striker of the year, gets the glamour of the group of fourth seeds.

So on comes the defender to draw the second seeds. Rangers are first out, for argument's sake, and you are thinking they can go in any of the eight groups. But then the old man from UEFA says 'and of course Rangers can only go in group B with Real Madrid'. Eh? They can only go in group B when eight are available. This will be for reasons of television or other countries or Real have asked to play a Scottish team, something like that. The defender is now massively confused and spends the rest of his part of the draw with a puzzled look on his face. At the same time as he is drawing teams, a UEFA minion is picking out balls to represent the groups a side could go into. These are normally drawn by a foot-balling legend, who is stood next to the UEFA old bloke harking back to the days when this competition was just a straight knockout.

The UEFA old bloke is looking smug, though. He is the only person on planet Earth who knows how this whole thing works. He has also been working on his pronunciation for months, so that when the Romanian champions pop out he is word perfect. He could be a native of Bucharest. Our mate Pedro will try to get in at the earliest opportunity to show that he can pronounce the Romanian team just as well. Every team is written on the piece of paper within a ball as they are known in their native country. This always provokes a great camera shot of a contingent from an English club wondering who the hell they have just drawn. 'Who are the exotic Girondins de Bordeaux that have just been plonked in our group?' you can see some of them thinking. Then somebody with a less insular mentality in the row in front lets them know it is just Bordeaux, and they can relax. Bayern München? What trip into the unknown are we embarking on here? Oh, don't panic, it's Bayern Munich.

About two hours after it started, it comes to an end. You feel drained, they all look drained. But everybody has got through it. All that has to be done now is for 'UEFA's special computer' to work out the fixtures, again based on their special rules. These special rules include this one: any English club drawn to play a Russian or Ukrainian side must play away to them in December when they will freeze their tits off.

When you move up a level to the draws for a World Cup or a European Championship, things get less complicated because there are fewer rules. For example, it's a bit tricky to draw somebody from the same country in one of these. However, they go on for longer because they are more officious – they require more men in blazers, and more committees – there are more videos about how great the host country is going to be, and there is also some obscure entertainment. A World Cup draw would be so much less of an event without Ricky Martin doing a star turn before it commences. All the national coaches and their association bosses couldn't possibly find out their tournament opponents before enjoying a bit of *la vida loca*.

And of course Sepp Blatter has to be there at some point, wittering on in some pointless speech. Given his past history he'd do better dressing up as Frank N Furter and doing a *Rocky Horror* medley for his less than adoring audience.

THE
MEDIA

The Phone-In

When I first wrote out a plan for this book – yes, it was planned – it looked like this was going to be the biggest chapter. It might still be. I won't know until I have finished writing it. I am trying to work out whether it could be so long because I work in the media and therefore know something about it and know what annoys me. Or is it because the media has become this giant behemoth that has expanded over the last twenty years and now dominates every aspect of our game? I am fairly sure the answer lies somewhere in between. Either way, it should mean there is plenty of material for the next few pages. And let's start with the biggest bugbear of the modern football manager. The thing they hate more than anything else.

Very occasionally, very very occasionally, I get recognized. It normally happens in the back of a taxi, and the conversation always follows the same pattern.

'Your voice sounds familiar.'

'Yeah, I do some stuff on the radio,' I reply, trying to be as vague as possible.

'Who do you work for?'

'The BBC, mainly Radio One and Five Live.'

'Well, I haven't listened to Radio One since DLT left, so it won't be that.'

A pause.

'That's it, you present 606, don't you?'

'I have done, yes. On and off. Since around 2002 actually.'

Another pause.

'I loved Danny Baker when he presented that show. He was great, wasn't he? Easily the best presenter that show has ever had. It was funny when he did it, wasn't it? Good stories and stuff, and he is a proper fan. Now it's just people moaning. Moan, moan, moan. That's all they do now. Why do they moan so much? Danny made it funny. I can't stand people who moan. And most of the other presenters have been crap, haven't they? I mean, David Mellor. David bloody Mellor. What did he know about football? I didn't mind Littlejohn, he was OK. I agreed with him a lot. Most of the presenters since then I have never heard of. Just a whole load of people who let people come on and moan to them. They probably aren't even fans, they are just celebrities. Never heard of them. What's your name again then, son?'

'Mark Chapman.'

'Oh yeah, right. I have heard of you. Didn't you shoot John Lennon?'

And all the time I just sit there in the back of the cab, nodding along in agreement. Well, not nodding along to the last bit. I was only seven when John Lennon was shot so it definitely wasn't me. I nod because I agree with a lot of what he is saying, but not all of it. The thing I agree with most is that Danny was the best, is the best. None of us since has come close to emulating what he did. A few of us have tried. I have tried, but it is never quite the same, because over the years the football phone-in has become the perfect vehicle for fans to moan.

When Danny started, it wasn't. It was fresh and new and there wasn't a plethora of football phone-ins around. His 606 was the only one. Here was a platform where we could all talk football. Here was a show we could be part of. And here was something we could listen to on the long journey home rather than trying to find a cassette to pop in after we had heard *Sports Report*.

I had never heard of somebody finding a dead dog at a football ground, or somebody's dad being hit in the face by a ball that Brian Kilcline had cleared into touch, or a fan's tortuous two-week journey home from a European tie in the Soviet Union. Now I have heard them hundreds of times over. Every self-respecting talk radio station has to have at least one football phone-in, which means the same stories get told over and over and over again, often by the same people.

In the eight years of being involved with the programme, I've had only a couple of callers whose anecdotes I hadn't heard before and I can still remember. I once had a season ticket holder at Elland Road on the line who had missed Leeds beating Manchester United. The reason was he had bet his mate in the pub the night before that he could get to the game on his lawn mower. It was an eight-mile journey and halfway through it he ran out of petrol. I also spent a good proportion of one show discussing with one woman the perils of ordering a ham and pineapple pizza on a football tour to Eastern Europe. Apart from them, you can guarantee that the show will more often than not follow a pattern similar to this:

Presenter: Welcome to 606. We're here till eight o'clock tonight so plenty of time to get your call in. The number is 0500 909 693, and we'll start with Simon in Devon.

Simon in Devon: Hello. Rafa Benitez should be sacked. Liverpool shouldn't be drawing at home to Spurs. We won't win the title . . .

The Presenter will argue this point with Simon in Devon for a few minutes before it's on to the next caller.

Alex in Romford: I am really annoyed with how West Ham are playing. I can see us being relegated if we continue playing like this. I don't want to criticize Gianfranco Zola and say he ought to be sacked like that Liverpool fan was on about with Benitez, but he has to sort it out.

Presenter: Let's move on to Michael in Sunderland.

Michael in Sunderland: The referee today was awful.

Presenter: What game?

Michael: The Sunderland game. He didn't give us seven penalties, he missed two offsides for them, and he booked three of our players but none of theirs.

Presenter: But you lost 5–1 at home to Arsenal. That can't be the referee's fault.

Michael: Well no, but he wasn't very good.

Presenter: What was he called?

Michael: Can't remember.

Presenter: OK, thanks, Michael. That's two minutes of my life I won't get back. Tom is in St Helens.

Tom in St Helens: I can't believe what that first bloke was going on about. Get rid of Benitez? He must be mad. I go to all the home games and we were just unlucky today. Where was he from? Devon? He's not even a proper fan. Liverpool fans don't talk with that accent.

There will now follow some texts and two more calls from 'genuine' Liverpool fans, i.e. those with a Scouse accent, all criticizing the bloke from Devon.

Presenter: OK, let's move it on. Just time for one more call before the news here on Five Live, and Barbara is in Hereford.

Barbara in Hereford: I just want to say that all these fans just have no idea. They all support these big clubs and that isn't a struggle. A struggle is supporting Hereford. We are struggling for money and struggling to stay in the league. We are under real pressure. They ought to try coming and supporting us for a few weeks.

Presenter: I understand that, but you can't criticize them for Liverpool being their club.

Barbara: But we are really struggling.

Presenter: I know you are, but that isn't the Liverpool fans' fault. And just because they are worried about qualifying for Europe doesn't make your concerns more valid than theirs.

Barbara: But they should support their local team.

Presenter: A lot of them do. Here's the news.

A few swigs of my tea during the three or four minutes of news and sport and we are ready to go again.

Presenter: So, we have already talked West Ham, Liverpool, Hereford and referees tonight, but whatever you want to talk about, give us a ring now. Tom is on his way back from Stoke's game at Old Trafford.

Tom: Yeah, I just want to say, Mike—

Presenter: It's Mark.

Tom: Well, whatever, it's not as good since Danny Baker stopped doing it, but anyhow, Mac, I just want to say that the United fans today were dreadful. They were so quiet. Even though we lost 8–0, had two men sent off and our goalkeeper carried off with a badly broken leg, we never stopped singing and chanting. They were a disgrace. They were so quiet, and none of them are from Manchester.

Presenter: OK, Tom, thank you. Here's another Tom. You're an Ipswich fan, yeah, Tom?

Tom in Ipswich: Yeah, but I just want to defend referees after the bloke slagged them off earlier. They are just doing their best and players and managers need to show them respect. We all make mistakes.

Presenter: Are you a referee yourself, Tom?

Tom: I am, yep, and I just think they are doing a really good job.

Presenter: OK. Well, thanks very much for your call. Next it's—

Tom: Sorry, Mick—

Presenter: It's Mark.

Tom: Yeah, can I just say one more thing?

And at this point your heart leaps. It is the one phrase designed to fill a phone-in host with dread, particularly a football phone-in host. 'Can I just say one more thing?' It sounds harmless and it is harmless, but – and this is a big but – not when you do a football phone-in.

It's David Mellor's fault. When he hosted 606, he had a caller who made his point and then finished with 'Can I just say one more thing?' Mellor allowed him to. At which point the bloke went 'You are a . . .' and called him the worst swear word ever invented. It is a sentiment that is hard to disagree with, but the bloke was cut off. Mellor apologized and then said something along the lines of 'Well, he was a bit of a berk himself'.

So my heart is in my mouth. I am waiting for my Mellor moment, because, let's be honest, there are a lot of people who think I am a berk. But Tom will just say, 'I think Ipswich will do well this year.' And I will breathe another sigh of relief, and get through the rest of the show as fans of big clubs moan, referees get stick, and fans of smaller clubs moan while also taking the moral high ground over the fans of the big clubs.

Have you ever met anybody who has phoned a football phone-in? I haven't. Never. I have met people who have told me they were going to ring up and then didn't, but I've never actually met, face to face, a fan who has phoned up. I do wonder if there is a call centre somewhere of one hundred people who are good at regional accents and had numerous fresh anecdotes back in the day but who now just have to have a good moan every Saturday and Sunday night.

As the humorous stories decreased and the number of phone-ins increased, the space for fans to come on and criticize and moan became greater. Referees, managers, referees, players, referees, other fans and referees were all fair game. After years of only being able to criticize as a collective in a crowd, supporters now had a chance to have their individual voice heard. And as a society we do like a good moan. Why be positive and praise somebody or something when we can have a pop instead?

However, I absolutely love doing it. You know what to expect before the show has even started, yet it is still a lot of fun to do. It is just a chance to talk football, and what is wrong with that? There is a snobbishness when it comes to people discussing phone-ins. They get hammered by the people who work in football. Managers and players don't like them, which I can understand to a certain extent: they are the professionals and they are being criticized by amateurs. But phone-ins also get hammered on the internet. I tried to do a bit of research to find out the year when the caller abused David Mellor, but when I Googled it, it just brought up site after site that talked about 606. There were lots of messageboards that were critical of it. The irony of messageboards criticizing phone-ins will probably be lost on the majority of people who post.

And there is one other group of people that likes to slag off the phone-in. The football journalists. I have read numerous articles that have questioned the very existence of 606. The gist is often that fans don't know a great deal about the workings of the game and should keep their opinions to themselves. These views tend to crop up in what are known as 'opinion pieces' or 'columns'. This is where the journalist in question is given a page of the newspaper to pour out his thoughts, often critical, on the world of football. Again, Alanis Morissette could have used this situation for lyrical inspiration. It is certainly more ironic than rain on your wedding day.

We all have opinions, we all have thoughts, and we are all perfectly entitled to criticize anybody or anything, so I do not have any problems with journalists having a pop at me or the shows I work on. However, there is one thing that football journalists do that does cause me problems.

Journalists' Exclusives!

There is an uneasy relationship between the various factions of the footballing media. The television guys are seen as getting all the glamour, the newspaper guys are perceived as the ones who get the stories and have the contacts, and the radio guys are seen as the ones who take the stories from the newspapers, put them on air and get greater exposure for them. In a nutshell, the newspaper journos put in the hard graft, the TV and radio ones don't.

I had never considered these different dynamics when I was thrown into the mix of it all at my first tournament in Euro 2000. And it was hard. I felt very much like an outsider, and although I enjoyed the football, the tournament and Belgium – and not many people can say that – on a professional level it was hard. By Japan in 2002, things had changed for the better and I was part of the travelling England media entourage. This meant I spent a lot of time with the newspaper journalists, and whereas I'd felt excluded at the turn of the millennium, I felt included in the land of the Rising Sun.

In the newspaper game, when you become the chief football correspondent of a newspaper, you are referred to as a Number One. So at these tournaments, when all the chief football correspondents get together they are referred to as the Number Ones. (Not by everybody, admittedly. Several radio people use more derogatory collective nouns.) With the title of Number One comes a certain amount of prestige. Number Ones have better contacts, they are granted more access to managers and players, they have a slightly more impressive cut of suit – although in the world of journalism that isn't too difficult – and they get invited into Jimmy Hill's kitchen on a Sunday morning to talk football. Or they used to. They now appear to be sat in a big-headed bloke's penthouse suite. They are no longer just journalists, they are celebrities in the football world.

The Number Ones in Belgium were older, mistrustful and downright rude. A few of the old ignorant crusties remained by the time we got to Japan, but there was a new guard as well. Henry Winter, Shaun Custis, Matt Dickinson, Ian McGarry, Rob Beasley, Paul McCarthy and Andy Dunn were just a few who made that trip incredibly memorable. Friendly, nice blokes, who liked a beer and, in the case of Henry, the karaoke. They wrote for different publications but there wasn't competition between them, or if there was I didn't see it. However, the newspaper world is cut-throat, which is why – and this is my big bugbear – every single back-page story seems to have EXCLUSIVE splashed all over it.

Before I go any further, I am going to look up 'exclusive' in the dictionary. Bear with me.

exclusive a. & n. 1. High-class, expensive, not to be had. 2. Not published elsewhere.

Well, I am shocked, because that isn't what I was expecting at all. I was sure it was going to read

exclusive a. & n. 1. Attached to a newspaper story, usually a football one, that appears in at least three other papers as well as the one you are reading that morning. 2. Attached to a newspaper story, usually a football one, that states the bloody obvious. 3. Attached to a newspaper story, usually a football one, that has been around for ages, that everybody knows about, and that wasn't really a story in the first place.

This isn't the journalists' fault. The blame lies with the people who put the paper together, who want their publication to appear bigger, better and more on the money than those of their rivals. There are more stories on the back page of a tabloid that have 'exclusive' attached to them than don't nowadays. 'Mark Hughes Unhappy at Defeat – Exclusive', 'Carlo Ancelotti Learning English at Chelsea – Exclusive', 'Michael Owen Picks Up Injury – Exclusive'. But every single newspaper will have the same stories. I am wondering whether 'exclusive' has actually become code in the journalism world for 'no shit, Sherlock'.

Occasionally, there are proper exclusives. A proper story that nobody else will have got. But the reader will miss it because we are bombarded with exclusives on a daily basis.

David Conn in the *Guardian* often has exclusives. I think

this is because he is a red-hot investigative journalist and also because a lot of the subjects he investigates are so complicated that nobody else goes near them. They are worthy, though. He often writes on football finance and administration, and some of his revelations are startling, although I admit to struggling to understand quite a lot of them. Occasionally he is deemed worthy enough to have 'exclusive' splashed across his story and you can guarantee that it will be exclusive. It won't also be appearing on the back page of the *Sun* and the *Star*.

The Number Ones don't have the time to do what Conn does. Their world is a never-ending one of travelling, watching football, typing on laptops and meeting contacts, and what a bloody great world that is. They all meet the same people, they all watch the same games, they all get tips on the same stories. Their writing stands for itself. They don't need everything to be exclusive, and neither do we.

If you are smirking at the moment, thinking, 'What a brown noser, what an arse licker, praising all his mates in the press and saying their writing is good,' then stop right now. You want to disagree with me that their writing is good? Really? Have you taken a look at your own club's website recently?

Club Media

I never lived in the former Soviet Union – this book is full of startling revelations, I know – and therefore do not know what it would have been like to work for *Pravda*. I can only imagine that working for the state-controlled Communist newspaper would have been akin to working for a football club's in-house television channel or website in twenty-first-century Britain. In between swigs of vodka, Boris Yeltsin shut down *Pravda* during his presidency of Russia. It was probably one of the few decent things that he did, because by the time he left office his approval rating among the Russian people was down to 2 per cent. And by some quirk of fate, that is the same rating most clubs' own media gets from its fans.

Have you ever tried to get anything useful off your own club's website? Something interesting, something to do with your side that you care about? It is impossible. A latest injury update on a key player maybe, the real reason why somebody has handed in a transfer request, or a player's thoughts on why he has been dropped or is out of form. Maybe your club is in the process of being taken over, so you want the latest on that. Perhaps they are without a manager so you want to know who might be in the running, or a big transfer target has gone somewhere else so you want to know how that happened, and if somebody else is being lined up. If you want to know the answers to any of these kind of questions then for God's sake don't log on to your own club's website.

I am writing this part of the book just a week or so after Kevin Keegan won a case for unfair dismissal against Newcastle United. The club came out of the ruling quite badly and Keegan won around £2 million in compensation. It was a big story. It was all over the TV, radio, newspapers and the internet. The hearing took place in London, so it might have taken a while for news to reach the North-East, but it was barely mentioned on the official Newcastle United website. There was a quick line saying the club would make no comment and then a link to the official report and verdict. Nothing else. The main issue why Keegan left was control of transfer policy. If I was a Newcastle fan, I would want to know more about this policy. Has it now changed, and who is in control of it? I would feel I deserved an explanation for my club's behaviour and would want some indication of how they are going to progress, yet I got nothing from its official mouthpiece.

If I log on to manutd.com at this very moment, I can buy tickets for the home game with Bolton, I can read about Ryan Giggs winning the website's player of the month award, I can win various things courtesy of all the different sponsors. I can, of course, buy hospitality packages and turn the language of the site into Arabic or Japanese. I can also look at John O'Shea's favourite ten photos of his time at United, and who wouldn't want to do that? Can I find out what the injury to Ben Foster is that has kept him out of the England squad? Can I arse. But 'club news' does tell me that I can park for free at Old Trafford on matchdays if I drive an Audi. What a relief that is.

On the positive side, most websites are great for finding out about the up-and-coming players at the club. They all tend to have comprehensive coverage of the reserves and youth teams. If they win. If they lose, it is a little bit harder to find the information. A big win is plastered all over the home page; a defeat and it is in a corner, about three links in.

The clubs would argue it is their website, about their business, and it is their rules and they can do whatever they want and write about whatever they want. And who would own their own website and then write bad things about themselves on it? So it's a justifiable argument, except the websites and the TV channels are increasingly becoming the only way to find out about your club. The manager and the players will talk to them rather than other outlets, for two reasons. Firstly, they are contractually obliged to do so, and secondly, they know they won't get a rough ride from the person asking the questions. The club is the common cause whereas nasty journalists from elsewhere might try and catch them out or be critical.

I have written elsewhere about the dangers of in-house club television criticizing the manager or the team, Alex Ferguson having banned MUTV on a couple of occasions when pundits or presenters have got a bit too chippy. Everything has to be positive. There can be no negativity, even if you are a guest on the channel.

I have appeared on MUTV a couple of times, and the positivity required was not a problem for someone with such a sunny disposition as myself. I have even appeared on Liverpool TV, although my disposition might not have been as sunny during that interview. I was probably sunnier than all the Liverpool fans watching at the time, all seven of them, when they discovered a Manc on their Scouse-only station. Before appearing on either of them, I always checked what I could say and what I couldn't say because I didn't want the people working on the shows to end up getting into trouble with the club.

There are dedicated, intelligent and competent people working on these TV channels. They are often young and just starting out in their careers and there is an enthusiasm among them that you don't get in the cynical, downtrodden world of mainstream television. Yet they are not allowed to be too creative for fear of annoying their paymasters, the club. They have to think like the club would think, or want them to think, or they could get the sack.

Before my first appearance, I checked with everyone at MUTV that I could criticize the club's decision to take the words 'football club' off their badge. They agreed, eventually, that it would be OK. It wasn't popular, but it didn't get anybody into trouble. After my second appearance, I got to know better a couple of the lads who worked there and stayed in email contact. We would quite often discuss United and their form, but I started to notice that if I said anything off message about the team or a player, they wouldn't refer to it in their email back. I eventually twigged that they couldn't criticize the form of Nani, for instance, because they were on an official Manchester United email. Once we were communicating via private email, they could slag him off to their hearts' content. Only joking, if somebody high up in United is reading this!

Club TV channels, like club websites, are invaluable for taking you deeper into your club. You can watch the reserves and the youth team and discover the players of the club's future. It is also fun to delve into the past and watch classic matches, and catch up with former players and your heroes and find out just how much they have piled it on since they stopped playing. It is like diving into and submerging yourself in your own club's pick 'n' mix. Unfortunately, it is as sickly sweet as a pick 'n' mix as well. Everything, and I mean everything, about the club is great in TV channel world. There isn't a downside.

They all need a little bit of balance. What the Manchester United website and MUTV need is somebody to do what Boris Yeltsin did when he allowed free speech in his country for the first time. They need an elder statesman, an all-powerful being at the club who nobody argues with, who is experienced, grey-haired, with a ruddy complexion, and who likes the odd drink. If only they had such a character.

Press Officers

Of course, the real power at a club isn't held by the manager. Nor is it held by the board of directors, or even the chairman. No. The real power is in the hands of the club's press officer.

Or so the club's press officer likes to think.

I am sure the thinking behind the press officer's role was to facilitate the link between the manager and the players and the media. It turns out that the role is simply to make the life of any journalist or presenter as uncomfortable as possible.

Footballers, more often than not, are lovely to interview and a pleasure to chat to. Press officers, more often than not, are pains in the arse. Nothing is too little trouble for them.

I don't want this little section to be a 'woe is me', haven't these people been horrible to me, etc., etc., bit, because that would be self-pitying crap, and also these people, if I am too critical, might stop me getting interviews ever again. Instead, I would like it to be a plea to them. Smile, be friendly and try to help, not hinder. Deep down, I reckon you are all nice people. You think you have to be tough and cold and sour-faced because that is what is expected of you. You have to show you're tough and hard and uncompromising with the media because the players will respect you for that. If you can keep us waiting an hour and a half for an interview, then interrupt it several times to complain about questions, the players will think you are a tough cookie and will be on your side. You are allowed to show your teeth to us, in a smiling not a snarling way, but you don't have to bawl us out every couple of months to show your mettle. CJ in *The West Wing* isn't horrible to everybody, in fact she can be utterly charming. And yes, I am aware she is a fictitious character, but she will have to do to prove my point.

I think I will leave it there because you can't really be that interested in the relationship between press officers and journalists. But, next time you are watching a press conference and you see somebody interrupt a journalist and say he can't ask that question, then remember this little rant. And if you are a press officer reading this, next time let's have a group hug and smile at one another before you start tearing my questions to shreds.

Sky Sports News

Having got that off my chest – and boy, do I feel better for it – it is time to pay homage to one of the two greatest channels on the box. ESPN Classic is my second favourite station. I love sitting there for hours watching old sport. I lie in bed with the missus who struggles to understand why I am watching a re-run of Arsenal winning the title at Liverpool in 1989 at half past midnight. It seems obvious to me.

However much I love ESPN Classic, though, it is not the channel I turn to first when I pop the telly on. It is not the channel I have on now, as background noise, as I write this. Oh no. The Daddy of the TV world is Sky Sports News. Where would football be, indeed where would television be, without round-the-clock sports news delivered by one stunning woman and a bloke sat next to her who can't believe his luck?

I have always considered myself to have the best job in the world. Over the years I have managed to combine presenting sport on radio and television with a bit of music presenting on Radio One. It may sound a cliché, but never once has it felt like actual work. Over the past couple of years, I have had to change my mind. Dave Jones, Ian Payne, Jim White et al. have the best jobs in the world. 'Just let me get this straight, Jonesy,' I once said to Jones (well, it wouldn't have been Payne with that nickname, would it? His is Payney, and I assume White's is Whitey), 'you get paid to sit there daily and read and talk about football for four hours. And you're not just sat there on your own. You are sat next to bloomin' Georgie Thompson or Natalie Sawyer who you get to flirt – sorry, banter with for four hours at a time. It's a hard life.'

Allow me to digress for a short time here, please, to offer a personal apology to Georgie Thompson. At the same time as she was presenting the sports news with Jonesy every afternoon, I was on Radio One presenting with Scott Mills. Jonesy had the better deal. Scott knew that I was an admirer of Georgie, in a professional way of course, and decided to bring this conversation to the air. This particular afternoon she was wearing a white shirt with a massive collar. It looked like a Harry Hill cast-off. I made the slight error of mentioning this on air to Scott. That afternoon, Sky Sports News received approximately four thousand texts and emails mentioning Georgie's shirt. At that moment, my chances disappeared. Although it was only in my head that I had a chance! Shortly after that, Georgie hooked up with good-looking, funny, multi-millionaire nation's sweetheart Declan Donnelly from Ant and Dec. You can't blame her, can you?

Texts and emails are a huge part of Sky Sports News, as they are for most television and radio shows. Where would we be without knowing that George in Middlesbrough thinks Middlesbrough are great, or Trisha in Ipswich doesn't like Norwich, or Scott in Southampton thinks there is a touch of the Harry Hill about Georgie this afternoon? But it's not the interactivity that SSN deserves the most credit for, it is their ability to treat sport like the most serious thing on earth, which is something we should be grateful for.

There is so much information for the viewer to digest on the screen on SSN, from club fixtures, league tables and leading goalscorers on the right to all the day's stories broken down into a couple of sentences along the bottom. You can read all of these while the presenters are delivering different stories in the main box. However, the real excitement comes when the small thin bar that moves horizontally across the bottom of the screen turns yellow. This signifies breaking sports news. Just to emphasize that, 'BREAKING NEWS' in big black letters appears on the thin yellow strip. Your heart starts to beat that little bit faster. What you are about to see on the screen could make or break your day. Is this the moment when Rafa Benitez gets the sack? Have Manchester City smashed the transfer record to sign Cristiano Ronaldo from Real Madrid? You move close to the screen and get ready to see the words as they move across.

PETERBOROUGH UNITED RESERVE STRIKER BEN
WRIGHT INJURES ANKLE IN TRAINING.

It comes as something of an anti-climax. Unless you are a Peterborough fan, of course, in which case it is quite interesting news, or indeed if you are the friends or family of Ben Wright. As easy as it is to laugh at the absurdity of a reserve striker's injury at whatever level being a matter of breaking news on a national channel, there is a huge part of me that loves the fact they take football so seriously that it is essential to include every little bit of football news from around the country, however small.

There is another reason why every single bit of football news is included, however small: Sky own the rights to all the domestic competitions and therefore they can get access to the people involved, have footage to show, and can promote their upcoming coverage. Sports they don't own the rights to barely get a look in, and it is hilarious in the summer to watch that yellow breaking news strip tell us about the Peterborough reserve striker while at the same time ignoring the fact that Rafael Nadal has beaten Andy Murray at Wimbledon or that Lewis Hamilton has won the British Grand Prix.

The rights issue does create slight problems during World Cups and European Championships. It is easy to ignore other sports because SSN is predominantly a football news station. But when the two biggest football tournaments on earth are in progress and Sky don't own the rights, they have a massive dilemma. There might be one minute on the battle between Theo Walcott and Aaron Lennon for the place on the right wing for England's next game, followed by a good five minutes on how Hartlepool's pre-season is looking.

I am not sure I would be very good on SSN. Many would say I am not very good on anything. It is that self-deprecating side of my nature that wouldn't really fit in, plus I would laugh too much at how serious everything is.

At England press conferences there was always a set order of who would ask the questions. Nick Collins from SSN would sit in the middle of the front row, moustache bristling, and would always, always, ask the first two or three questions. He was Sky's man, and with that came the prestige of going first. The message was that he was the England guru. When you watched coverage of the press conference on SSN and always saw him with the first few questions, you realized he was the man.

All of their men and women out in the field give that impression on screen. Their reporters stand outside grounds day in, day out, often in the pouring rain, claiming little scoops here and little scoops there. They have received a text from this chairman, or that manager. This player gave them a ring last night about a story, or, in the case of the cutting-edge younger reporters, they received a tweet. I was watching once when David Craig was stood outside St James's Park and he said he had received a text from somebody on the club board and they were going to send him out some cakes or sandwiches because he had been out there a long time. How connected does that make him sound? Craig is so important on the North-East circuit that the clubs are willing to feed him. I can't remember what the story was about, all I can remember is that he was going to get food.

I have a feeling that it happened on transfer deadline day,

and as we all know, the final hours of transfer deadline day on SSN is the funniest sitcom on television since *Phoenix Nights*. Jim White, a Scottish, tanned, greying presenter who is not averse to hyperbole, conducts the proceedings, with a bit of totty on one side of him and a bloke called Andy Burton on the other side. Andy is like a Del Boy for the twenty-first century. He sits in the studio surrounded by mobile phones, BlackBerries and, the last time I saw him do it, a pager. I didn't know anybody still used pagers. Somebody other than Andy must, because the stories were flying in on it. I don't know how Andy does it, because when you have mobiles near microphones and other broadcasting equipment there is a horrible buzzing sound whenever they are about to ring or get a text. Yet you never hear any of that, which is impressive. Jim's role is to ask Andy what stories he is getting, what rumours he is hearing, and to talk to all their reporters outside training grounds trying to see who is coming and going. He is also contractually obliged to mention Sky Sports News every thirty seconds. Rumours start and are then denied. If I didn't know better I would suggest that the odd rumour was started deliberately so that you heard it first on SSN and then heard it denied first on SSN.

It is breathless, it is exciting, it is tremendous television that has you laughing out loud, and at the end of it the biggest transfer has been a player moving from Luton to West Brom on a season-long loan. But it doesn't matter. Transfer deadline day used to pass with minimum excitement and with minimum fuss. Now it is great fun, has great energy, and is treated as seriously as proper news channels treat a Cabinet reshuffle.

Yes, SSN is a little bit self-important and takes itself too seriously, and yes, it does ignore a lot of sport just because it is on the BBC, but it is addictive and it is informative. Oh yeah, and it has gorgeous women on it.

Pundits

Sky Sports News isn't my favourite Sky product – and this isn't going to be a Sky love-in. Far from it. The best thing that Sky do is the cricket. Their coverage is superb. Cricket as a sport is very lucky to be as well covered as it is. *Test Match Special* on BBC Radio Four is an iconic programme with the highest standards, and when the sport was shown on Channel 4 the coverage was similarly excellent. The secret to all this success was the quality of punditry. The thoughts of the experts used are intelligent, insightful and humorous. It is difficult to say the same thing when discussing football.

Michael Atherton, Nasser Hussain, David Lloyd, Geoffrey Boycott, Phil Tufnell and Alec Stewart are just some of the ex-players who work across the cricketing media. Not one of them holds back on what they think. They praise when it is justified and they criticize when it is required. There is no such thing as sitting on the fence. Their playing days are behind them and their responsibility is now to their viewers and listeners. They are not beholden to the current England team and they have to be brutally honest. They know it might not make them incredibly popular among the modern-day players but that is the price they have to pay for moving from the middle into the commentary box.

This honesty doesn't happen in football. Punditry in football is more often than not bland. It is words for words' sake. If a football pundit can sit on the fence, he will. It is better to do that than cause offence. The blame for this doesn't lie solely with the football pundits, it more often than not lies with the current players and the clubs. If a pundit is critical on either television or radio, their station could be banned, as I mentioned earlier, but the pundit himself could also suffer. Be critical of his former club and the pundit might be banned from club events, club dinners, testimonials, and hosting corporate guests at league games or on European nights. They could be blackballed by the very place where they gave distinguished service. And if your heart isn't exactly bleeding for them at that prospect, then remember that for the older players, the ones who didn't earn millions of pounds, these dinners and club events are a good way to earn money.

A sport gets the pundits it deserves. Football, in the main, gets bland expertise because it is too childish to cope with anything else. I have headed to a cricket ground on the morning of an international reading Michael Atherton in *The Times* questioning the greatness of Andrew Flintoff as a cricketer. I am thinking, 'Blimey, Athers, he is going to go for you next time he sees you.' I then arrive at the ground to find Atherton and Flintoff having a laugh and a giggle out in the middle. Cricketers might get the hump every now and then but they don't hold on to grudges for years and years like people do in football.

It is us, the fans, who are getting short-changed in all of this. As well as being opinionated, the pundits are meant to be there to educate. When you watch the cricket coverage you feel like you are learning all the time. John McEnroe educates you as you watch Wimbledon, Martin Brundle does the same for Formula One. Andy Gray for football? Do me a favour. 'Take a booow, son' and all that nonsense. Explain things to me, tell me about formations and tactics and the best way to deal with certain players, or what kind of team talk might be required at half-time for any given situation, rather than coming up with catchphrases to become some kind of cult (feel free to make a typo error, Mr Publisher) hero on *Soccer AM*. And while we're at it, Mr Gray, would you mind referring to all players by their surnames? At the moment you refer to the ones you want to be friends with as Stevie, Frank, John and Wayne and the rest by their surnames. One rule for the multi-millionaire England foot-ballers and another for the Titus Brambles of this world is what it seems like to me.

Cricket, tennis and Formula One are in essence more complicated sports and therefore it is easier for a pundit to educate. But there is a laziness among a lot of our pundits. 'He'll be disappointed with that,' one will say as a striker balloons a penalty over the bar. Really? 'He's got to get closer to him than that,' another will explain as a centre-half is ten yards away from a centre-forward when he scores. Well blow me, I hadn't thought of that. With all the technology avail-able now, the arrows on the screen and the squirly circles underneath players, we should be doing better than that, shouldn't we?

Is football too simple? Does it need to be more complicated in order to get better pundits? Not really. Football pundits just need to look more at Lee Dixon, who is the best football expert on television, and Stewart Robson, who is the best pundit I have worked with. Both, unfortunately, have links with Arsenal, but you can't have everything. Dixon is eloquent, amusing, and really searches out different aspects of a match to show you in his analysis. He points out things the ordinary fan wouldn't notice. It is probably no coincidence that he played under Arsène Wenger and has brought that kind of intelligence to his punditry.

Robson was a midfielder for Arsenal and West Ham in the 1980s and isn't the best-known footballer of his generation. He worked with me quite a lot when I presented Italian Football for Channel Five. He was sometimes in the commentary box and sometimes in the studio and was always insightful when it came to tactics, formations and how to defend. Mind you, as that show was presented by me and an Italian model with little grasp of English and even less of football, it wasn't hard to appear witty, urbane and intelligent. Laura Esposto and I had less chemistry than Sam Fox and Mick Fleetwood hosting the Brits.

So, both Dixon and Robson show it is possible to keep up with cricket and tennis and Formula One when it comes to expertise. The football community just needs to realize that criticism comes with the territory and it is never personal. Hopefully, Andy Gray will think like that if he ever reads this section.

Fantasy Football

So, I am sat watching a Premier League game on a Sunday afternoon with a mate. Liverpool are away to Arsenal, and my friend is a Gooner. It is a difficult fixture for me because I feel dirty cheering for either side. I always need a good shower afterwards. My mate is happy as the full-time whistle approaches with Arsenal three goals to the good after a sensational performance. The three points they will garner means they are still in the title race. Life is good for them, and for him.

Then, with a minute to go, Yossi Benayoun threads a through-ball to Fernando Torres. The Spanish striker is clear of the Arsenal back four. He is away. His pace takes him into the penalty area. There is only Manuel Almunia to beat. It will be a consolation goal, no more. He looks up. He picks his spot and slides it past his countryman in goal. The net remains as still and as motionless as a lake on a cool, wind-free day. Torres has slid the ball past Almunia but also past the post. It stays 3–0 to Arsenal.

My friend – a Gooner, let's not forget – has his head in his hands. 'How did he miss that?' he asks.

'Because he looks like a girl,' is my reply. 'Why does it bother you? You're going to win. Why have you got your head in your hands, you nob?' Even at this late stage in the book, there is still room for the odd nob mention.

'Because Yossi Benayoun is in my fantasy team and that assist would have got me three points.'

Jesus wept. He is willing to watch his own team concede a goal for the sake of three points in a make-believe world. And, not Fernando Torres in his Fantasy Football team but Yossi Benayoun.

I remember when Fantasy Football first came out. It wasn't linked to a newspaper at the time. You had to send off for a pack, and when it arrived, it was like finding the Holy Grail. This was my chance, and my friends' chance, to be football managers. The nearest any of us had got to it was playing a game called *Football Manager* on the ZX Spectrum 48. *Championship Manager* it was not. Hi-tech it was not. Being in charge of some stick men trying to score in five-a-side goals was not the same as managing real top-flight footballers.

With high anticipation, nine friends came round to my mum and dad's house one evening, and with a can of Boddingtons each (oh yeah, I knew how to entertain) we began the auction. All top-flight players were up for grabs. Each one would be offered up for sale, and if you wanted him you had to make a bid. None of us really knew what we were doing. One friend's season was over before it had even started as he spent three million on Brett Angell and had very little to allocate for the rest of his squad.

At the end of a long night, with several beers drunk, nine of us had squads we were pleased with and one of us had Brett Angell and a load of reserves. Now we had to manage these players and try to win our fantasy league. By 'manage', of course, I just mean select the team and occasionally swap players around. It was nothing more complex than that.

By Christmas, eight of us had completely forgotten to switch players around and the only two people doing it week in, week out and taking it seriously were the two people fighting it out at the top of the league. I wasn't one of them.

It became huge, and it was turned into a television series – Fantasy Football as a whole, I mean, not me and my mates' league. It was presented by Frank Skinner and David Baddiel, and for the first time ever football was seen as entertainment rather than just sport. The programme made football funny, it made famous people into football fans, and it made Jason Lee's life hell.

As well as the TV series, newspapers fought over the format, so that now we are at the stage where nearly every single daily paper has some kind of Fantasy Football league. All of them are fairly similar, bar one, where rather than a Fantasy Football manager you can be a Fantasy Football chairman, which sounds dreadfully dull. You get the chance to pretend to sit on board meetings, pretend to fall out with your manager and pretend to saddle your club with billions of pounds' worth of debt, I assume.

The proliferation of these competitions means that they are all trying to outdo one another. The prizes are greater for winning it but the scoring systems have become more complicated. It is ten points for a goal scored by your player, unless it comes off his right knee between the 53rd and 58th minutes in which case you get twelve points. A yellow card is minus three points, unless the player received it for a foul on Joey Barton, in which case they get one hundred points for your team. It has become too complex.

'How thick must he be to find Fantasy Football too complicated?' you must be thinking. That isn't my main problem with it. My main problem is that I just can't be arsed with it. I have tried. Every now and then I am prepared to give it a go. I start with great enthusiasm and carefully mould my squad, but like in my first ever season of Fantasy Football, I just forget about it. I have better things to do on a Friday night, like have a curry and watch telly, than fiddle about with my squad online. Also, I resent how it changes your views on what is going on in the real world of football, just like my mate at the beginning. On the odd occasion I have done it, I have ended up wanting Liverpool to keep a clean sheet because, for financial reasons, I had to include Emiliano Insua as my left-back. I have urged Cesc Fabregas to curl in a last-minute free kick at Everton because he was my midfield lynchpin alongside Sean Davis from Bolton (again, for financial reasons). Plus, my mate had Tim Howard in goal so it would screw up his weekend if Howard let one in. Grown men end up doubting their allegiances because of some made-up game.

It is wrong, and it should stop now so we can all get back to supporting our own teams in the real world.

DVDs

Have you seen that one where the goalkeeper goes to throw the ball out to his defenders but gets it wrong and somehow ends up throwing the ball into his own net? How about the one where the defender, right on his own line, tries to clear the ball but instead smashes it into the top corner? Or, what about the really camp referee who prances all over the pitch, often in pink, and has a particularly flamboyant way of brandishing red and yellow cards? Of course you have. You have seen them all, over and over and over again, on every single bloody DVD that comes on to the market, or on those hilarious sporting clips shows on the television.

Gaffes, clangers, howlers, cock-ups, own-goals, shockers, blunders, blinders – all words that can appear on the front of a DVD together with the obligatory footballing celebrity in comedy scarf, hat or kit, and make your heart sink. Hilarious the first time, still funny the second, third, even fourth time, but tiresome and tedious by the tenth time, and I could be talking about either the clips or the number of DVDs around. They are all the bloody same. How many times can they be repackaged with a different presenter? Ray Winstone, Danny Baker, Lovejoy, Ricky Tomlinson, Ricky Hatton, Rory McGrath, Paddy McGuiness, Ian Wright, Gary Lineker, Danny Dyer, James Nesbitt, John Motson, Adrian Chiles, David James and Johnny Vaughan have all laughed all the way to the bank by fronting the same old clipfest.

And if you don't buy the DVD you can always catch a clips show on television. They tend not to have a presenter but instead rely on lots of amusing celebrities to talk about the clips. Alex Ferguson and Brian Kidd dancing on the Old Trafford pitch after a late comeback against Sheffield Wednesday is sadly lacking something until it is put together with Kate Thornton's thoughts on the two Steve Bruce headers that won the game. I am ashamed to say I have taken the shilling and done the odd one or two of these. I annoy myself if I ever see these programmes. I add absolutely nothing at all to them and most of them were filmed when I was going through a strange phase and had blond highlights. I thought it would give me extra lift; in fact I just look like Audrey Roberts from *Coronation Street* talking about the treble-winning season.

Clips shows and gaffe-prone DVDs presented by middle-aged celebrity fans need to stop now. There should be a fifteen-year amnesty during which people can hand in all their copies with no questions asked. 'Yes, you bought a Johnny Vaughan football DVD, let's leave it there and move on. We all do things we regret. In time it will be forgotten and you will be forgiven.' At the same time as all this crap is being handed in, no more clips shows can be broadcast or made. Then, in fifteen years' time, we will have a whole new selection of gaffes and howlers, plus the ones we have seen incessantly for the past fifteen years will have the warmth of nostalgia around them. They can all be put together on a DVD and presented by Tinchy Stryder or Cheryl Cole who will both be middle-aged enough to present it by then.

Books

What every single category in this chapter illustrates, and the DVDs section in particular, is that football allows a lot of people to make a lot of money out of it. As well as the DVDs, there is one other mass-market way people try to earn a few bob out of the beautiful game. Books.

On the subject of football, they are everywhere. From players' biographies to weird and wonderful facts, from tackling the serious matters confronting the modern game to hilarious list books, they take up a lot of shelf space, or if you are modern and buy online, a lot of webpages. If you are writing a football book then you have to fight to get yourself noticed. This was obviously near the top of the pile in the reduced bin when you saw it, so that's a relief.

A lot of the books are crafted with care and attention and, more importantly, with a feel and a love for the game. Others are just banged out there to earn a few quid and a famous name is plonked on the front cover to get it to sell. There is no problem with that. All of these books we devour, or we should devour, to improve our knowledge of the game and the people involved in it. You can't go wrong with a list book because it gives you hours and hours of things to argue about down the pub when you have all read it. I did consider doing a list book as well, but it is tricky to come up with a list that hasn't already been done. 50 Best Footballers, 50 Worst Footballers, 50 Fattest Footballers, 50 Thickest Footballers, 50 Footballers Whose Mother Was Called Doris – they have all been done. I should know, because whereas I refuse to own a bloopers DVD, I do have football books piled high in my house.

There is one type of football book that I refuse to buy. These are the worst kind. The ones that just criticize everyone and everything to do with the game. There is a prime example of this kind of literature, and I do not want to give this one particular book any publicity whatsoever, but I need to bring your attention to the hypocrisy of it.

It was written by a journalist who had covered both football and cricket during his career. In recent years he had stopped writing about football because he didn't like the way the game had gone. He decided there were a good deal of people to blame for him not liking the game any more so he wrote a book about them, slagging the lot of them off. Obviously he was too canny to describe his piece of work as a 'slagging'. He used the word 'lament'.

It is exactly the kind of football book that makes me so angry. No longer in love with the game, a dislike of so many people connected with the game, a willingness to criticize a wide range of people who have given so much to the game, yet happy to try and make a few quid out of the game and out of those same people. If somebody isn't in love with a sport, why write about it? Why criticize some of the legends of the game, some of whom are no longer with us and therefore can't answer back? Could it be to get some publicity so that you sell more copies and make more money?

If you are going to piggy-back football and try to earn a living out of it in some way, either by writing or broadcasting about it, then I think you should show a bit of gratitude towards the sport and the game and not be so lamentable.

So, thank you to the players. Thank you to the kit manufacturers, the people who make the balls and the WAGs. Thank you to Graham Kelly and the people who put the FA Cup draws together. Thank you to the club websites and the players who wear hairbands. Thank you to Newcastle fans, and to Newcastle United FC and their placement of away fans. Thank you to stroppy managers, 4th officials, the FIFA committee that introduced squad numbers and the newspaper workers who add 'exclusive' to every story. Thank you to the designers of football grounds, the hosts of phone-ins, the makers of headsets, the wearers of headsets, the footballers of Aylesbury and Georgie Thompson. And thank you to every single person who pays their hard-earned money to go week in, week out to watch football. Without the fans, nobody at all, not even the players, would make a living out of the greatest game on earth.

And if that paragraph has had you reaching for the sick bucket, then just read it back once again, a little more carefully this time. Note that I haven't thanked either Sepp Blatter or anyone connected with the official England Band. That is because they are still nobs.

Epilogue

Dear Ben,

I had no idea when I began to write this book how it would turn out. Would I get angrier and angrier as I wrote? Would I rant and rave over and over again? Would I be confronted with a sport that just infuriates me every year older I get, or would I find some redeeming features in it? I have got angry as I have written it, I suppose I have ranted and raved at times, but I am not left with a feeling of hate towards the game.

You are too young to understand this at the moment, son, but I have come to the conclusion that football is very much like living with your mother. There are ups and downs, there are very good times and very bad times, and every year that goes by we infuriate each other a little more. But there is a love there that is very special. It is a love that can only come from years in each other's company, that can cope with the lows and the highs we both experience, that is incredibly deep. A love that if it were missing would make life incredibly hard. That is how I feel about football. Your mother comes just below that feeling.

Football has given me the most amazing life, and I hope it continues to do so. It has, in essence, given me a career, for which I will always be grateful. If I was hit by a bus now, then it would be my own fault for trying to write on a laptop while crossing a road, but I would die knowing that I had worked for Radio One, Five Live, BBC Sport and ESPN and presented shows on all those networks, including some of the biggest in the business, from breakfast on Radio One to *Final Score* on BBC1. This isn't a boast, just an indication of job satisfaction and of achieving some of the dreams I had when I was a little bit older than you. I have never sat next to Georgie Thompson, but you can't have everything, and if I avoid being hit by buses for the next couple of decades then who knows?

But my work and my jobs don't really matter that much compared to everything else football has given me. It has given me moments of pure joy, it has given me shared experiences that only fellow football lovers can understand, and it has given me the best friends a man can ever wish for.

The non-believers will claim that I could have had similar friends if theatre had been my love and not football. That may be true, except we wouldn't have sat around for hours talking football in the pub, we would have spent hours pretending to be trees or talking with jazz hands. Although, obviously, if you do decide to be an actor, I will of course support you. Unless you ever do jazz hands, in which case I will disown you faster than it takes Cristiano Ronaldo to run fifty yards.

I am still in touch with the boys I went to United with that first ever time. My central defensive partner for seven school years, Sutts, will still claim to this day that he did all my running for me and I just stood there and headed it away, and he will pray that every time we meet I don't retell the story of my one and only goal for the school, which was a forty-yard top-corner screamer against our biggest rivals. At some stage you will meet the back four from my university days, and you too, like everybody from the days at Hull, will shake your head and wonder how a back four of Bone, Williams, Chapman and Plows managed to keep any strikers at bay. We were lighter and quicker in the early nineties, although admittedly still crap.

It doesn't matter how long it is between us seeing each other, we carry on where we left off. We have a shared bond that nobody can break. We were a team, a unit. Only we know what went on in the changing rooms, only we know what went on on the coach trips, only we can remember the great victories and the heartbreaking defeats. I still maintain I wasn't responsible for a quarter-final defeat at Newcastle, and I still have to apologize to our goalkeeper's dad for launching a stream of abuse at him the first time he ever came to watch us because I assumed he was with the opposition.

And now you come and watch me, still trying to play as forty gets ever closer. One of the disadvantages of not having children when you are nineteen is that your kids don't get to see you at your physical peak. Having said that, your mother would be furious if you got a girl knocked up at that age, so don't do it. I feel slightly embarrassed as you watch me lumber around the pitch, trying to get involved. I once scored when you were there, but you weren't watching because you had gone for a wee behind a tree.

But as you watch your dad struggle for breath, touch, pace and skill, I hope you also see the spirit between the lads. The will to win is there, the passion and the commitment is there, but so is the fun. There is laughter and desire and there is a determination to enjoy what for most of us is the best ninety minutes of the week. We are able to run on to a pitch covered in turds, with holes in the nets, three instead of four corner flags and a referee who is seventy-two and feel like we are Manchester United, pretend we are Rooney and Ferdinand. Because that feeling never goes. You might think you will grow out of trying to be your heroes. You never do, and you never should.

You have learnt very quickly that the comedy character in our Saturday side is Boney. I have now been in the same side as Boney for nearly twenty years, through university, through a Sunday league side and into this Saturday side. If you find somebody like Boney through playing football then you will be a very lucky boy. He is ageing, he is greying, and to put it kindly he has made the best of his limited foot-balling ability, but we have never laughed as much as we do playing football. We go to games together, we go for beers together – to talk football, obviously – we laugh at each other on the pitch and we shout a lot at each other on the pitch as well. He understands me, I understand him, and without football I wouldn't have one of the greatest friendships of my life. Plus, he has the worst first touch of anybody I have ever seen, so he always makes me feel better about myself.

There is one person I haven't mentioned in all this talk of friendships and camaraderie and that is my dad, your Grandpa. The man who first took me to Old Trafford. My earliest memory is jumping all over him while he tried to watch the 1978 World Cup Final. My best memory is standing in the Nou Camp with him in 1999. Dad had deliberated long and hard about whether he would come to the Champions League Final between Manchester United and Bayern Munich, because he had a lot of work on. After a lot of persuading, he decided to come with me. We arrived early and sat in our seats in the top tier in the sun, drinking a beer and watching the Nou Camp fill up. It was a beautiful sight.

The game was not the best – as you know, because when your mum went out when you were still a baby I used to put you in your playpen and stick a re-run of the match on the telly for us both to watch. So, you remember when Teddy Sheringham scored? Well, at that point I was jumping around. And you remember when Ole scored? Well, at that point I was hugging anybody near me while still jumping around. And then you remember when the final whistle went? Well, then I stopped jumping around. Then, I turned to your Grandpa and hugged him and burst into tears. It was the end of an eighteen-year journey for us. It made all the years of watching Ralph Milne and Terry Gibson worth it. It made thumping home defeats by QPR as a way to welcome in the New Year feel like a drop in the ocean. This was what me and Dad had been waiting for. Going to United was our thing, nobody else's. Father and son together in defeat and victory, and now, in the warmth of a Catalan night, our dream had come true. I cried as much for that as for actually winning the blooming thing.

I thought I had never seen Dad happier, but that wouldn't be true. Remember that forty-yard screamer I scored for school? Your Grandpa jumped so high when that went in he nearly ended up in a tree. He had watched me week in, week out for seven years. Wherever I played, he was there. (Granny wasn't, because when I was thirteen she came to watch dressed in a cagoule and a coat and moon boots. The embarrassment was so great, I asked her not to come again.) He had never seen me score. And then I went and did that. Forty yards, top corner, bang. I don't remember how I celebrated, I just remember him having to extricate himself from branches.

I thought he was going mad, but now I understand his reaction perfectly, because I am now in his situation and you are in mine. Except you, you little smartarse, scored in your first competitive game. I have never celebrated a goal as loudly or as deliriously in my life. My little boy, slotting home. I can't remember when I felt so proud. I always thought the phrase 'bursting with pride' was ridiculous, but on that Sunday morning I understood it. As I nearly ended up in a tree and your mum burst into tears, you ran off celebrating with your team-mates. Already you are experiencing the joys of being in a football team. You have your little friends, you want to play for them, tackle for them and win for them. There is not another feeling like it.

I watched with pride as you took the captain's armband, and when you couldn't get it on your scrawny little arm you put it on your leg like some kind of garter, my pride slightly tempered by the thought that you could be a cross-dresser. I watched you cajole your team, I watched you run your little heart out – I am afraid you have inherited your dad's pace – I watched you smile, laugh and shout, and I witnessed the pain that only a footballer can feel when a goal is conceded. And I thought back to my own childhood, and I thought how lucky you are to be at the start of your footballing journey.

As I sit here now and look at the tickets from my first game in front of me on the wall, if I turn to the left then I see other mementos that make me smile, and I am not talking about the signed picture of Katy Perry. I am talking about the pictures of you. You are in football kit in every one of them. You are heading a ball, kicking a ball, you are holding the FA Cup, and at a trophy presentation you are picking up the most improved player award. In all of them you are smiling, except the action photos, where you are concentrating intently.

The joy you are getting from football is evident. I can see it every day with you and all your friends. It is now the responsibility of my generation to ensure that this joy continues throughout your life. Football isn't more important than life and death, but it is precious, and it needs looking after. We need to make sure that you and your counterparts can play it, can afford to watch it, and can enjoy every facet of it. If you don't then we will have failed to protect the greatest sport in the world. I promise you that I will do all I can, despite having no influence whatsoever in the game at the highest level.

Powerless I may be, but, son, I will be with you every step of the way. I will watch you, I will cheer you, and I will take you to as many games as I can, and I hope that one day you and I will experience our own Nou Camp moment. The game will annoy you, it will frustrate you, but it will give you more enjoyment than you could ever think possible. You will make friends for life, you will have memories for life, you will love it and you will hate it, but you will always be grateful it is in your life. You will have heroes, of course. As your temperament is like your old man's you will have hissy fits most definitely. But if you ever, ever wear a hairband, I won't be responsible for my actions.

Have fun with the beautiful game, Ben.

Love,
Dad

Index

accents, fan 160–1
Adams, Tony 136
Adebayor, Emmanuel 128
Admiral England world kit 11
advertising boards, moving
    93–7
Aldridge, John 124
Allardyce, Sam 191, 197,
    199–200, 201
Allison, Malcolm 183, 194–5
amateur referees 211–13
Ancelotti, Carlo 183–4
Arsenal 105, 109, 147
    'Captain Call' system 18–19
    home strip (2008/09) 16
Ashley, Mike 162
Astle, Jeff 26–7
Aston Villa 176
Atherton, Michael 276, 277
Atkinson, Ron 183, 194
autobiographies, player 61–4
away fans, and grounds 82–8
Aylesbury United Football Club,
    goal celebration 124, 126–8

Baddiel, David 282
Baggio, Roberto 65
Bailey, Gary 2, 39
Baker, Danny 250, 251
Ball, Alan 41, 195
Ballack, Michael 120
Baros, Milan 66, 67
Barton, Joey 61–2
BBC, Ferguson's feud with
    191–2
Beardsley, Peter 68
Beasley, Rob 259
Beattie, James 14
Bebeto 125
Beckham, David 15, 36, 42, 55,
    56, 69, 110, 130
Beckham, Victoria 56, 59
beer, sale of at football grounds
    89–90
Benitez, Rafael 105, 184
Berbatov, Dimitar 12, 37–8
Bergkamp, Dennis 65
Berry, George 3
Best, George 38, 69

Bhoularouz, Khalid 68
Birmingham 85
Blackburn Rovers 232
Blackmore, Clayton 50
Blatter, Sepp 218, 223–30, 246,
    289
Bolton 200
Bond, Nigel 49
Boney 293–4
books, football 287–9 *see also*
    autobiographies, player
boots, football 40–4
    colour of 41–2
    personalization of 42–3
Boruc, Artur 109
Borussia Dortmund 77
Boycott, Geoffrey 276
Bradford City fire 154
Bramble, Titus 131
Brazil
    Confederations Cup match
        against Egypt (2009) 218
    goal celebrations in World
        Cup (1994) 124–6
    World Cup match against
        Ghana (2006) 76
Bremner, Billy 38
Bright, Mark 80
Brooking, Trevor 66, 67
Brooklands Youth FC 17–18
Brown, Phil 198, 201
Bruce, Steve 136
Brundle, Martin 278
Budweiser 90
Buffon, Gianluigi 69–70
bureaucracy 226

burglaries 55
Burton, Andy 274
Busst, David 119–20

Cahill, Tim 131
Campbell, Darren 50
Campbell, Sol 68
Campo, Ivan 200
Cantona, Eric 32, 36, 67, 69, 130
Carragher, Jamie 68
Celebrity Soccer Six tournament
    40
Champion, Jon 76
Champions League 136
    draw 242–6
    Final (1999) 294
chants, fan 149–55
Charles, Prince 78–9
Charlton, Bobby 38
Chelsea 29, 84, 147, 232
    Community Shield match
        against Manchester United
        120
Clemence, Ray 66
Clough, Brian 175–6, 183, 196,
    203
club chairmen 176, 178 *see also*
    owners, football clubs
clubs *see* football clubs
CNN 243
Cole, Ashley 62–3
Cole, Cheryl 59
Coleman, David 214–15
Collins, Nick 273
committees
    and FIFA 225–7

and UEFA 227–8, 242
Conn, David 260–1
consumerism of football 233–4
Cook, Gary 93, 235
Coppell, Steve 69
Coronation Street 52
Corrigan, Joe 66
Coyle, Owen 196
Craig, David 273
cricket 217, 276–7
Crotty, Dick 17–18
Crouch, Peter 130–1
Custis, Shaun 259

Dabo, Ousmane 61
Dalglish, Kenny 68
Davies, David 240
Deayton, Angus 50
Deschamps, Didier 54
Di Canio, Paolo 119, 120, 131
Diaby, Abou 68
Dickinson, Matt 259
Director of Football 175
diving 101, 103–4, 108–14
Dixon, Lee 279
Djemba-Djemba, Eric 33
Djorkaeff, Youri 200
Dossena, Andrea 68
dugouts 216
Dunn, Andy 259
DVDs 284–6

Eagles, Chris 39
Eduardo 109, 110, 111, 113, 114, 119
Edwards, Martin 176

Egypt, Confederations Cup match against Brazil 218
electronic boards 219–20
Elleray, David 209–10, 222, 223
England Band 168–71, 289
England kit launch 14–15
Eriksson, Sven-Göran 58
ESPN Classic 269
Esposto, Laura 279
Everton 16, 90, 96
Evra, Patrice 120, 183

FA Cup draw 239–42
FA Cup Finals 134
  (1981) 134
FA Cup games 85
fans 143–8
  accents of 160–1
  chants 149–55
  England Band 168–71, 289
  and football phone-ins 249–57
  grounds and away 82–8
  importance of kits 16
  Newcastle 161, 162–7
  portrayal of in media 149–50
  quietness of home crowd 145–7
  showing them in tears 165–6
  tourist 156–61
  as vital component of football 143
Fantasy Football 280–3
Ferdinand, Rio 62

Ferguson, Sir Alex 105, 110–11,
    183
  feud with BBC 191–2
  Keegan's rant against 186
  and MUTV 192–3, 264–5
  and Ronaldo's move to Real
    Madrid 229
Ferguson, Jason 192
FIFA 116, 118, 225
  and committees 225–7
  see also Blatter, Sepp
Finnan, Steve 68
First Division, winners of 232
Flintoff, Andrew 130, 277
Foé, Marc-Vivien 69
Follas, Matt 29
food and drink, sale of at
    football grounds 89–92
football clubs
  at heart of community 94
  singing sections 147
  TV channels 264–6
  websites 262–3
Football Manager (computer
    game) 70–1
football tragedies, chants about
    153–5
footballs 22–8
  colour of 24–6
  goalkeepers complaints about
    new 27
  leather 26–7
  Nike Total 90 Omni Ball 23–4
  and science 23–4
Forlan, Diego 14, 129
Foster, Steve 38–9

4th official 216–22
Fowler, Robbie 129, 131–2
Frankfurt's stadium 78
free kicks 103–4
Fritz-Walter-Stadion (Germany)
    77–8
Gallagher, Noel 166
Gallas, William 65, 72
Gascoigne, Paul 12, 67, 128
George, Charlie 38
George, Finidi 131
Germany
  hosting of World Cup (2006)
    76
  stadia 76–8
Gerrard, Paul 119
Gerrard, Steven 62, 105, 110,
    184
Giggs, Ryan 48
Gillingham 106
goal celebrations 124–33
goalkeepers
  complaints about new
    footballs 27
  fans abuse of 86
Goodison Park 83, 90
Goram, Andy 151
Gray, Andy 278
Greenwood, Ron 66–7
grounds, football
  away sections 82–8
  food and drink on sale at
    89–92
  moving advertising boards
    93–7
  see also stadia

Haaland, Alf Inge 107
hairbands 35–9
Hansen, Alan 136
hardman 107
Hart, Paul 196
Hartson, John 13
Hawthorns ground 80
headgear, and managers 195
headsets
  and managers 199–203
  and referees 213–15
Henry, Thierry 31–2
Hillsborough disaster 154
Hoddle, Glenn 66, 67
Hodgson, Roy 180
Holland, World Cup match
    against Brazil (1994) 124–5
Houllier, Gérard 132
houses, players' 51–7
Hughton, Chris 162
Hull University FC 20, 292
Hunter, Norman 112
Hussain, Nasser 276

Ibis FC 20–1, 70
Ince, Paul 20, 107
injuries 115–23
inner shirts 13–14
interviews, with managers
    185–8, 190
Irwin, Denis 144

Japan, hosting of World Cup
    (2002) 75–6
Jennings, Andrew, *Foul! The
    Secret World of FIFA* 225

Johnson, Andy 131
Johnstone's Paint Trophy 239
Jones, Dave 270
Jones, Vinnie 12
journalists, football
    criticism of phone-ins 256–7
    exclusives 258–61

Kappa 13
Keane, Robbie 68–9, 131
Keane, Roy 36, 107, 210
    'prawn sandwich' comment 90,
      159
Keegan, Kevin 38, 66, 68, 162
    'I would love it' rant 186
    as manager of Newcastle 163,
      164
    wins unfair dismissal case
      against Newcastle 263
Kelly, Gary 131
Kelly, Graham 239–40
Kewell, Harry 68
Kilcline, Brian 136
Kinnear, Joe 162
kiss-and-tells 59–60
kit, football 11–16
    importance to fans 16
    inner shirts 13–14
    launches of 14–16
    marketing of 11–12
    scientific claims 12, 19–20
    skin-tight shirts 13
    socks 29–34
    trends in 12–13
    wearing skins 19–21
Klinsmann, Jürgen 130

Kobe Port Earthquake Memorial Park (Japan) 76

Lampard, Frank 62
Lawton, Tommy 26–7
Lee, Francis 111–12
Lee, Sammy 201
Lerner, Randy 176
Linighan, Andy 134
list books 287–8
Liverpool 68–9, 85, 150
Liverpool TV 265
Livorno 69
Lloyd, David 276
London 156–8
London Marathon 168
Louganis, Greg 108
Lua Lua, Lomano 131
Lucarelli, Cristiano 69

Mabbutt, Gary 136
McAteer, Jason 49
McCarthy, Mick 196
McCarthy, Paul 259
McEnroe, John 278
McGarry, Ian 259
McIlroy, Sammy 3
McMahon, Steve 107
Madejski Stadium 79
managers 177
  dress sense 194–8
  and headsets 199–203
  and media bans 189–93
  and owners 177
  pre- and post-match
    interviews 185–8, 190

and press conferences 179–84, 273
shadow cast over game by reactions of 105–6
Manchester City 93, 232
  attendances 164, 165
  retiring shirt numbers 69
Manchester United 2–5, 36, 144, 160
  and Champions League Final (1999) 294
  Community Shield match against Chelsea 120
  number 7 shirt 68, 69
  seating of away fans at Old Trafford 83
  signing of Robson 3
  website 263–4
Maradona, Diego 65
Mariner, Paul 66, 67
Match of the Day 2
Match, The 48
Materazzi, Marco 218
Matthews, Stanley 26–7
Maxwell, Robert 176
Mazinho 125
media
  ban on by managers 189–93
  books 287–9
  and clubs 262–6
  DVDs 284–6
  Fantasy Football 280–3
  journalists' exclusives 258–61
  not talking to by referees 221–2
  phone-ins 249–57

and press officers 267–8
pundits 276–9
Sky Sports News 269–75, 276
Mellor, David 250, 255
Mikoliunas, Saulius 113, 114
Milla, Roger 131
Mills, Scott 270
minute applause 151–2
minute silences 151
Moore, Bobby 69, 135
Moses, Remi 3
Motson, John 135
Mourinho, José 68, 85, 197
Moyes, David 179, 180
Murray, Colin 96
MUTV 192–3, 264–6

Nani 24, 131
Neville, Gary 187
Neville, Phil 51–2, 54, 55–6, 104–5
Nevin, Pat 96
Newcastle United 217, 263
  (2008/09) season 162
  attendances 164–5
  fans 161, 162–7
  stadium 87–8
  website 263
newspaper exclusives 258–61
NFL 232–3
Nike
  and skin-tight shirt 13–14
  Total 90 Omni Ball 23–4
Number 10 shirt 65
Nürnberg stadium 78

Okocha, Jay Jay 200
Old Trafford 83
Oldham Athletic 143–4
O'Leary, David 41
Oliver, Michael 106
O'Neill, Martin 195–6
Owen, Michael 110
owners, football club 175–8
Oxford United 176

Panorama 192
Payne, Ian 270
Pearce, Stuart 30, 107
Pelé 65, 229
Perryman, Steve 136
Phelan, Mike 192
phone-ins 249–57
Pinto, Pedro 243
Pires, Robert 110
pitches, preparing for play in cold weather 25
Platini, Michel 65, 228
play-acting 115–16
players 50
  autobiographies 61–4
  earnings 6
  framed shirts 54–5
  houses of 51–7
  and injuries 115–23
  squad numbers 65–72
  WAGs of 58–60
Poll, Graham 64, 207–8, 213, 221
Portugal 58
'prawn sandwich' brigade 90, 159

Premier League 231–7
  clubs that have won title 231–2
  criticisms of 231–2
  television deal 233
  thirty-ninth game in season suggestion 234
Premier League All Stars 48–50
press conferences 179–84, 273
press officers 267–8
Pulis, Tony 195, 196
pundits 276–9
Puskas, Ferenc 65

Rangers 151
Ratcliffe, Kevin 136
Ravanelli, Fabrizio 129
Redknapp, Harry 179–80, 185, 191
referees 101, 103, 105, 116–17, 207–15
  amateur 211–13
  and Elleray 209–10, 222, 223
  fear cult amongst 105–6
  and headsets 213–15
  not allowed to talk to the media 221–2
  and Poll 64, 207–8, 213, 221
  schoolmasterly style 210–11
Reid, Peter 107
Rennie, Uriah 211
replica shirts 66
reporters, football match 185–7
Rivaldo 115–16, 118
Riverside stadium 79
Robson, Bobby 183
Robson, Bryan 3–5, 36, 67, 69, 95, 107, 136
Robson, Stewart 279
Rochdale 106
Romario 125
Ronaldo, Cristiano 5, 36, 69, 160
  and diving 110–11
  move to Real Madrid 229
  Neville tackle on 104–5
  Rooney incident in World Cup (2006) 58
Rooney, Wayne 5, 19, 58, 63, 110, 132, 183
rugby 103, 234–5

St James's Park (Newcastle) 87–8
Savage, Robbie 210
Schmeichel, Peter 120
Scholes, Paul 102
science
  and footballs 23–4
  and kits 12, 19–20
Scolari, Luis Felipe 58
Scotland 150–1
Scudamore, Richard 234, 237
Shackleton, Lee 175
Shankly, Bill 183
Sharpe, Lee 40–1, 50, 66, 67, 131
Shearer, Alan 127, 162, 164, 217
Shilton, Peter 66
shin pads 34
shirt numbers 65–72
shirts, football 12–14
  inner 13–14
  players' framed signed 54–5
  removal of in game 129
  replica 66

skin-tight 13
  wearing skins under 19–21
shorts, football 12
606 (radio programme) 250, 251, 252–5
skin-tight shirt 13
Skinner, Frank 282
skins 19–21
Sky Sports News (SSN) 269–75, 276
Smicer, Vladimir 68
Smith, Alan 131
socks, football 29–34
Souness, Graeme 107
Southgate, Gareth 197
sponsors 136–7, 139
Spoony, DJ 40
squad numbers 65–72
stadia 75–81
  in Germany 76–8
  lack of diversity in Britain 78–80
  Wembley 80, 136
  see also grounds
Stalteri, Paul 68
Stamford Bridge 84–5, 147
Stein, Jock 183
Stewart, Alec 276
stoppage time 220
Stubbs, Ray 127
Stuttgart ground 78
substitutions, and electronic boards 219–20
Sunderland 85, 147
swimming pools, indoor 53–4

tackling 101–7
Taylor, Graham 48, 179, 180
television
  club's in-house 264–6
  Premier League deal 233
Terry, John 29–30, 34, 68
Test Match Special (radio programme) 276
Tevez, Carlos 35–8
Thompson, Georgie 270
Torres, Fernando 105, 184
Touré, Kolo 65
tourist fans 156–61
tournament draws 238–46
  Champions League 242–6
  FA Cup 239–42
  types of 238–9
  World Cup 246
transfer deadline day 274–5
Traore, Djimi 150
trophy presentations 134–40
Tufnell, Phil 276

UEFA 96, 113–14, 243
  and Champions League draw 242–4
  committees and panels of 227–8, 242
UEFA Cup 96
under-seven matches 122–3
Unsal, Hakan 115–16

Valencia, Antonio 160
Van Nistelrooy, Ruud 110
Van Persie, Robin 106
Venables, Terry 183

Vermaelen, Thomas 65
Verón, Juan Sebastian 33
Vieira, Patrick 107
Villa Park 83
vox pops 161

WAGs 58–60
Webb, Howard 218, 221, 222
websites, club 262–4
Wembley
  demolishing of 136
  new stadium 80
Wenger, Arsène 68, 105, 108,
  110, 111
  chants about 153
West Ham 85
  retiring shirt numbers 69
Westfalenstadion (Dortmund)
  76–7
White Hart Lane 83

White, Jim 270, 274
Wilkins, Ray 39
win-at-all costs mentality 103,
  107
Winter, Henry 259
Winter, Jeff 211
Wise, Dennis 162
women's football 230
Woodcock, Tony 66, 67
World Cup
  (1982) 66
  (1994) 124–5
  (2002) 75–6
  (2006) 58, 62, 76–8, 218
World Cup draw 246
World Society of the Friends of
  Suspenders 230

Zamora, Bobby 150
Zidane, Zinedine 65, 218

Mark Chapman (aka Chappers) is a sports broadcaster, journalist and DJ. He is now presenting three weekly shows: *Talk of the Terrace* on ESPN, *Late Kick Off* on BBC 1 and his own new Monday evening show, the *Monday Night Club*, on BBC Radio 5 Live.

Chappers has regularly hosted BBC Radio 5 Live's *606* football phone-in, presented the Radio 1 *Drive Time* show with Scott Mills for ten years, and also teams up with his colleague Comedy Dave on the radio as well as for the university roadshow, the *Chappers and Dave World Tour*.

Chappers is one of the lead presenters on ESPN, including its Premier League coverage, and on the BBC, for whom he regularly hosts *Match of the Day Live* and *Final Score*. He has also anchored Five's European and Italian football coverage and the chart-topping *Chappers' Premier League Podcast*.

Mark lives in London and supports his hometown club, Manchester United.